I NEED ANSWERS

30 COMMONLY ASKED QUESTIONS ON MARRIAGE

DR GRACE SOLA-OLUDOYI

DIVINE
Flow
PUBLISHING

I dedicate this book to my best friend,

my encourager, my lover

PDSO, my hubby.

CONTENTS

Acknowledgments   9

Why I Wrote This Book   11

1.   I don't love my husband anymore.   15
What should I do?

2.   I feel lonely in my marriage. What do I do?   21

3.   How can a wife best communicate with her   25
husband who is experiencing fear?

4.   My wife is moody, reserved, and silent.   29
There is hardly any communication
between us, and when there is, it is volatile.

5.   Should I submit to my laid-back husband who   33
does not seem to have a vision for the family?

6.   My husband doesn't listen. What do I do?   41

7.   Why does my wife always nag?   45

8.   I don't like arguing with my husband, but it   49
happens a lot. What can I do to stop this?

9.   Should a woman always be the one to look after   55
the children at home while the husband works?

10.   I earn more than my husband. I can tell it is   59
causing him to resent me. There is tension
in our marriage that wasn't there before.
What do I do?

11. What should I do if my mother-in-law is undermining me? How do I get my husband to address it?   *63*

12. Is it alright for the husband to continue hanging out with his friends and go on men's outings as if they're still single?   *67*

13. Is this okay for a husband or wife to be communicating with his or her ex-with or without the knowledge of the other?   *69*

14. Why do we keep fighting over money issues?   *73*

15. Should Christian couples have prenups?   *79*

16. Is it good for a man to hide important information about his health, work and property from his wife and children?   *83*

17. I don't enjoy sex with my husband, and I don't know why. Can you help me?   *87*

18. My husband wants oral sex, but I am not sure if it's permitted before God. I want to please my husband; what do I do?   *91*

19. Can one have sex while fasting?   *95*

20. Can I have sex during my periods?   *97*

21. I secretly masturbate to release tension. I don't want to commit fornication. Am I sinning?   *103*

22. I am addicted to pornography.   *107*
How can I stop it?

23. My husband is impotent. I am sexually   *111*
frustrated. He refuses to get medical help
because of his ego. How do I deal with this?

24. Why did my husband have an affair?   *117*
Can my marriage survive it?

25. Is courtship for six months   *125*
enough to consider marriage?

26. Why should I not marry someone of a   *129*
different religion or who is irreligious?

27. I am in love with a guy who has AS genotype,   *133*
my genotype is AA. Should I be worried for
when we have children?

28. Do interracial and interethnic marriages work?   *139*

29. I am experiencing abuse in my marriage.   *145*
What do I do?

30. I am a 39-year-old Christian lady who   *169*
divorced five years ago. Can I remarry?

Conclusion   *175*
References   *177*
Other Books   *179*

ACKNOWLEDGMENTS

I wish to acknowledge and thank the hundreds of men and women who attended our various virtual marriage talks during the pandemic lockdown period. Your participation, positive feedback, testimonials, questions on Slido and Zoom chats informed the making of this book.

Special gratitude to all those I have been privileged to counsel through life's arduous journeys.

My heartfelt gratitude to all the numerous authors and writers whose books and articles helped to shape my insights, opinions, and views on the questions.

I want to thank every member of Royal Connections for your continuous prayers and support, and for being the medium through which my passion for marriage blossomed.

I am grateful to my PA, my armourbearers, and Royal Women Executives for all you do for me.

Thank you to my parents and siblings. Your encouragement and support always mean a lot to me.

I also say thank you to my invaluable hubby, PDSO, for being my best friend, my confidant, my inspiration and for travelling with me along the journey called life.

Thank you to my wonderful children - Sade, Enoch-David, and Mary-Grace, for being my most enthusiastic cheerleaders. Like I usually say, greatness awaits you.

To God be all the glory!

WHY I WROTE THIS BOOK

Thank you for choosing to read *I Need Answers: 30 Commonly Asked Questions on Marriage.*

You are either happily married, struggling in marriage, engaged to get married, desiring to get married someday, interested in marriage, out of marriage or simply curious about the contents of this book. Whatever the case, I hope you find it a valuable investment in your life and relationship.

The inspiration to write this book stems from the profound desire to build and strengthen marriages, solve some common problems in marriage, alleviate pain, suffering, and ignorance in relationships. Also, I hope to contribute what I can to make a difference in my generation and leave a legacy in marriage.

If there is an institution most attacked by the enemy today, it is the institution of marriage. Marriage is the first institution God made; it is a covenant relationship that binds a man and his wife together as one (*Genesis 2:18, 23-25*). Marriage, as God ordained, is intended to bring pleasure, fulfilment, favour, reward, and many blessings. Sadly, many marriages, including Christian marriages are not a testament to these. Divorce rates are high and as a result many children are growing up in broken homes.

Did God make a mistake creating the institution of marriage? Are His plans and purpose for the marriage institution already thwarted by the enemy?

Irreconcilable differences, 'grown apart', 'fell out of love', neglect and abandonment, are a few of the reasons given by couples as grounds for divorce and separation. All this ought not to be so.

Problems in marriage are part of our fallen world. I believe there is no marital problem that cannot be solved, especially if God is in the marriage.

This book gives carefully crafted answers to marital problems, and it is full of biblically-based insights, down-to-earth wisdom and well-researched knowledge of marriage dynamics.

Following a series of Marriage Relationship Talks held by my husband, Pastor David Sola Oludoyi (PDSO) and

I during the lockdown seasons in the pandemic year 2020, with countless testimonials received, it was laid upon my heart to pen down answers to some of the questions asked during the meetings. This book is the end product.

To do justice in answering these questions, I delved into thorough research for nine months. I availed myself of several resources including many relationships books, articles, and sermons. All these helped to inform my insights, opinions, and views on marriage.

Additionally, my years of clinical and ministerial experiences and my own marriage experiences lend weight to the answers inscribed on the pages of this book.

Some questions were not easy to answer, as there are different schools of thought, even amongst Christians, as the scriptures seem to be silent on some topics.

In answering the real-life questions tackled in this book, I have deliberately applied general principles rather than personal examples. This is because each marriage and the couples involved are unique, with their peculiar circumstances.

I understand that you may have some contrary opinions from mine in some answers. That is fine; nevertheless, I hope you will find many of the answers within this book beneficial.

May the Holy Spirit who guides us in all truth, guide and direct your decisions, and choices. May every page and chapter of this book enable you to acquire valuable insights, skills, and attitudes to help you prepare for, build, repair, restore, and strengthen your marriage.

Dr Grace Sola-Oludoyi

London, UK

I DON'T LOVE MY HUSBAND ANYMORE. WHAT SHOULD I DO?

There are many reasons for marital dissatisfaction; hence the root cause is worth exploring.

I'll start by asking you a few questions.

How long have you felt this way and has it gotten worse now?

Have there been any recent changes in your home?

Does your husband know how you feel towards him, or do you allow him to think that all is well?

Are you perhaps attracted to someone else?

If he doesn't know the extent of your dissatisfaction or what bothers you, it will be difficult for him to improve the relationship.

A lack of intimacy often develops after the arrival of children. They take energy, time and a lot of attention, which could easily make your husband get sidelined. One thing to realise is that you didn't just wake up one day feeling this way. The feelings have developed over time.

Working through the issue will also take time and patience.

Firstly, you need to address the issue by having a long and meaningful conversation with your husband. He may be wondering what is wrong and is afraid to ask you. Perhaps his ego is a bit bruised, or he feels the same as you do.

Knowing where each of you honestly stands is the first step towards change. Choose the right time to talk. Do not engage in what may be a sensitive discussion when any of you is tired, sad, or angry. Choose an uninterrupted quiet time together. Avoid confrontational talk, no blaming, no finger-pointing, and no shouting. Be gracious with your words.

Perhaps you need to rekindle the fire of romance in your marriage. You may need to date each other again. A date night once a month amidst your daily hustle can be a great boost for your relationship.

Think back to what attracted you to him in the first place. Note down his good qualities. Over the next month or two, endeavor to focus on all that is attractive in him rather than the little things that irritate you about him.

Search your heart. Is there a grudge? Did he do or say something or not say or do something and it hurt you? Have you discussed it with him or just brushed it under the carpet and let it fester? Do you feel unappreciated, and overwhelmed? Does he seem overcritical lately? Are you resentful towards him? Does he offer physical contact only when he wants sex?

Hormonal issues can affect a woman's sex drive and emotions. Are you struggling with depression or self-esteem issues? Consider seeing your doctor or counsellor.

Most couples go through rough times but if the difficulties last more than two years with no improvement, consider professional help, e.g. couple therapy.

It is also crucial for couples to understand all the ways their spouse says "I love you." Gary Chapman calls it "the love language".

In his book, *The 5 Love Languages, Gary Chapman* writes about the five ways people speak and understand emotional love.

He further writes that we must be willing to learn our spouse's primary language to be effective communicators of love.

These five languages are:

1. **Words of affirmation**, i.e., verbal compliments or words of appreciation. They are best expressed in simple, straightforward statements of affirmation, such as "you look sharp in that suit."
2. **Quality time**, i.e., giving someone your undivided attention. If your spouse's primary love language is quality time, she simply wants you to be with her and spend time together.
3. **Receiving gifts**, i.e., the receiver of gifts thrives on the love, thoughtfulness, and effort behind the gift. The gift itself is a visible symbol of love It doesn't matter whether it costs money. What is important to the receiver is that the spouse thought of him or her.
4. **Acts of service**, i.e., doing things you know your spouse would like you to do. You seek to please them by serving them, to express your love for them by doing things for them. They require thought, planning, time, effort, and energy.
5. **Physical touch**, i.e., a powerful vehicle for communicating marital love. Hugs, pats on the

back, holding hands, and thoughtful touches on the arm, shoulder, or face—they can all be ways to show excitement, concern, care, and love. For some individuals, physical touch is their primary love language. Without it, they feel unloved. With it, their emotional tank is filled, and they feel secure in the love of their spouse.

Adapted from The 5 Love Languages® by Gary Chapman, © 2015, Northfield Publishing, www.5lovelanguages.com.

Do you know the primary love language of your spouse? If not, identify your spouse's love language and embark on learning it. It will do wonders for your marriage.

I FEEL LONELY IN MY MARRIAGE. WHAT DO I DO?

Marriage does not necessarily insulate us from the grips of loneliness. Loneliness is determined by the subjective quality of our relationships, not their objective quantity, nor just by a couple living together. It often happens slowly as the disconnect we feel from our spouse gradually increases over the years.

Loneliness can be taxing both emotionally or physically, and it could come with depression, suicide, anxiety, low self-esteem, alcoholism, and drug abuse.

Conversations become purely transactional e.g. we need to pay the school fees, your sister called, did you pay the bills, or focused on parenting.

Couples can fall into daily routines that foster emotional distance, e.g. one spouse watches TV in the evening, the other is on the computer, or one sleeps at 10pm and wakes up at 5am, while the other goes to bed at midnight and wakes up at 7am. They lose the love and affection but stay in the marriage. Ironically, often it is out of the fear of being lonely, although by doing so, they potentially doom themselves to the loneliness they are trying to avoid.

It is also possible for a couple to eat together, sleep together, watch the TV together and parent together, but at the same time, feel alone. They may have sex, but the love is absent. There is talk but no real communication, connection and understanding. There is a feeling of exclusion, distance, and little intimacy.

When you feel alone, and you are both functioning as two separate entities, you often argue about silly things that are stand-in for deeper issues.

You may keep up appearances or go through the motions so you can appease your spouse.

You could possibly thrive in all other environments without having a closer relationship with your spouse, e.g., work, outside interests, with friends, etc.

If you don't deal with it, it festers on.

How to deal with loneliness:

1. Stop feeling sorry for yourself.
2. Communicate with your spouse and talk about how you feel e.g. *I feel a bit disconnected, and I want to be more connected. So, here are some suggestions.* You may have to help your spouse so that he/she can help you.
3. Try and understand their point of view; recall good times and have a laugh. Do small favours for each other.
4. Try something new; learn a new hobby and nurture yourself.
5. Reach out to others like friends and family. Have fun with them. Invite them over if possible.
6. Focus on your career and self-care.

HOW CAN A WIFE BEST COMMUNICATE WITH HER HUSBAND WHO IS EXPERIENCING FEAR?

Men are generally career-oriented and success driven. Their self-worth is intrinsically attached to work. The man who struggles in his career will often push away a woman who loves and cares about him, even if she wants to be supportive and doesn't care that he's not bringing home the biggest paycheque or climbing the ladder of corporate success.

The greatest fear of a man is that he is not good enough, or that he will fail.

Your response, initiative, and connection to your husband are crucial to the health of the marriage. Your expression of your unconditional love and acceptance is the very force that will drive you together amid the testing times in your marriage. Standing with him in the painful as well as good times is one of the primary elements of a great marriage.

Unconditional love is the commitment that says I will stay with you for better or for worse. I will always love you. I will affirm and support you.

Acceptance means I will love you even during tough times.

Putting aside your needs in order to meet his means a lot. Resisting your tendency to be selfish or self-protective and focusing on him matters.

Your husband desperately needs to know that you will accept him, even when he fails.

Your refusal to love can cripple or tear him apart. Your love will build him up. Giving your husband the security of your unwavering love requires at least five elements:

1. Show grace in his weaknesses. All of us need grace. If he has failed you or sinned against you, he needs your grace.
2. Affirm him whenever possible. Make statements like, "I am proud of you, love; you are such a blessing", etc.
3. Help him feel safe. Assure him that you do not intend to criticise him, but you are committed to him. Let him know that you want to help him work things through any patterns that could undermine the marriage's security. Just as a female feels understood when the husband

listens to her feelings, a husband feels better when the wife listens to his ideas.

4. Take time to connect with him.
5. Study your husband: Know him inside and out. Use your instincts to pick up what's going on with your husband, and what's going on in his head. Read his moves and moods. Timing is always important.

MY WIFE IS MOODY, RESERVED, AND SILENT. THERE IS HARDLY ANY COMMUNICATION BETWEEN US, AND WHEN THERE IS, IT IS VOLATILE.

Marriage is supposed to be that one safe place where you can be yourself and speak freely, but when you're afraid to communicate with your spouse, your relationship and home can feel like a prison.

The most vital ingredient in your relationship is communication. Communication is to the marriage, what blood is to the body.

The influence of one's upbringing is profound on a relationship's behaviour. Incidents of conflicts, violence and hostility in a family can negatively affect children's communication skills. As children grow into adulthood, their communication patterns often persist and can potentially impact their ability to communicate in their romantic relationships.

What makes people afraid to communicate?

1. They fear the risk of an argument or fight. They would rather not bring up unpleasant topics or areas of disagreement because they think their spouse will get defensive, angry or counter-attack them.

2. Insecurity, fear of rejection, chastisement, or abandonment if they share their feelings, fears, hopes and vulnerabilities.

While you may not want to stir up trouble or risk triggering your spouse's anger, staying quiet sets both you and your marriage up for failure.

There are lots of reasons why your wife may be moody. Your wife might not even know she is in a bad mood. Oftentimes those in a bad mood don't even realise they're acting out or taking it out on their loved ones. If it is out of character, it may be that she is going through a difficult time in her life, e.g. work, health etc. She may improve if the underlying issues are resolved.

She may be struggling with a deeper issue such as depression. Signs of depression include little energy and lack of motivation to do things she previously enjoyed, feeling miserable, loss of appetite, showing less interest in the children, keeping to herself, avoiding friends, avoiding housework, calling in sick at work, lack of interest in sex, and more.

Other causes of moodiness might stem from ongoing anxiety and unresolved issues with self-worth and low self-esteem.

If her moods are impacting on the relationship, it is important to talk about it. Find a time to talk when you're both in a better frame of mind, as it may be a difficult conversation to have. Show compassion, offer a listening ear. **James 1:19 (NKJV):** *"So then, my beloved brethren, let every man be swift to hear, slow to speak, slow to wrath";* and be empathic, **1 Peter 3:7 (NKJV):** *"Husbands, likewise, dwell with them with understanding, giving honor to the wife, as to the weaker vessel, and as being heirs together of the grace of life, that your prayers may not be hindered."* Learn communication skills and how to resolve conflicts. Be mindful of your non-verbal communication. An adage says *"communication is 10% what you say and 90% of how you say it."* Be considerate of both you and your relationship regarding timing and location of discussing sensitive topics.

If she is in a bad mood, ask her the following questions:

- Is there something I can do to make your day better?
- Do not ask what is wrong with her (this implies that there is something wrong with who she is).
- If she is telling you what is wrong, listen.
  Follow up with these questions: *Do you want me*

to just listen, or are you looking for comfort or advice?

- If she is upset and you have done all the above, and she is still responding with "I am fine", or "nothing", or silent treatment, try cheering her up by speaking her love language. Do you know her love language?
- Be patient. Give her time and space. She will come round.

For more tips on communication skills and how to resolve conflicts in marriage, refer to Question 8.

SHOULD I SUBMIT TO MY LAID-BACK HUSBAND WHO DOES NOT SEEM TO HAVE A VISION FOR THE FAMILY?

Ephesians 5:21-25,33 (NKJV): *"Submitting to one another in the fear of God, Wives, submit to your own husbands, as to the Lord. For the husband is head of the wife, as also Christ is head of the church; and He is the Savior of the body For the husband is the head of the wife, as also Christ is the head of the church; and He is the Saviour of the body. Therefore, just as the church is subject to Christ, so let the wives be to their own husbands in everything.*

Husbands, love your wives, just as Christ also loved the church and gave Himself for her, Nevertheless let each one of you in particular so love his own wife as himself, and let the wife see that she respects her husband."

Colossians 3:18-19 (NKJV): *"Wives, submit to your own husbands, as is fitting in the Lord. Husbands, love your wives and don't be bitter toward them."*

S ubmission in marriage always begins with mutual submission to Christ. **Ephesians 5:21 (NKJV):** *"submitting to one another in the fear of God."*

Submission is translated from the Greek word *hupatasso*, which means "to subordinate" or "to arrange under." Submission is a yielding experience; intelligent, humble obedience to an ordained authority. It goes hand in hand with respect and also an attitude of the heart. Submission is a voluntary selflessness to please God and obey His word.

The Bible teaches that in the Spirit, women are equal with men, and each must submit unto Jesus as their spiritual head. God, in His plan, has specifically asked wives to submit to their own husbands. In the marriage relationship, women are to be subject to their husband's headship. The Lord ordained that the man be the one that would make final decisions in the home, after consulting with his wife, because in any relationship involving two people, one must be the final authority. In the marriage, the man is the head and should guide his home and family. In the Spirit, Jesus Christ is the head of His family, and He guides each member according to His headship. Men are to love their wives like Jesus loves the Church. He laid His life down for her. Men who demand that their wives submit to them have not learned the right way to win them, and that is to love them with the love of the Lord.

In contemporary culture, submission is perceived as women being inferior to men, but that is not so!

Submitting to your husband's leadership in marriage is not hard if you marry the right kind of man. If you trust that your husband has your best interest in mind, and lays aside his own needs to love you specifically the way Christ loves the Church, why would you not submit to him? This is God's idea: "You and your husband both committed to putting the other one first in love." *Oludoyi, G (2015), I Pronounce You Husband and Wife!, Revised Edition, London: Baruch Press, 168-171*

Unfortunately, many marriages are less than ideal; hence, submission becomes an issue for both husband and wife. Many factors make women struggle with the concept of submission, from wounds developed in past relationships, to being manipulated in the name of submission and so on.

No husband should ever force his wife to submit to him through coercion or manipulation. Submission is her willing decision not only to follow him, but ultimately and supremely to follow in obedience to her Lord (Christ). Submission never requires a wife to follow her husband into sin. Her ultimate allegiance and loyalty are to Christ. If her husband abuses his God-given authority and requires of the wife something contrary to the God's word and will, she must obey God rather than her husband.

What submission is not: Submission to your husband does not mean a wife should be a silent, a 'yes' person, or agree with everything her husband says, or not have her own opinion; neither does it mean she gets her spiritual strength from her husband. He is not to maltreat, abuse, oppress, dominate, or disrespect his wife or treat her like a doormat.

In what ways can you submit to your husband?

1. Give him the responsibility of final decisions.

As his wife, share your view of things with him. If he disagrees, allow him the privilege to implement what he feels is right. Don't nag him about it; it can be counter-effective, and if you feel he is making a big mistake, why not talk to God about it? If you feel he needs your opinion and he's not asking for it, take a risk and give it. However, speak wisely and apply the law of kindness (**Proverbs 31:26 {NKJV}:** *"She opens her mouth with wisdom, and on her tongue is the law of kindness."*).

2. Respect and honour your husband.

Do this even when you feel he doesn't deserve it; after all, you are fulfilling your role because of your love and fear of God. **1 Peter 3:1-2 (AMP):** *"In the same way, you wives, be submissive to your own husbands [subordinate, not as inferior, but out of respect for the responsibilities entrusted to husbands and their accountability to God, and so* *partnering with them] so that even if some do not obey the word [of God], they may be won over [to Christ] without discussion by the godly lives of their wives,*

when they see your modest and respectful behavior [together with your devotion and appreciation—love your husband, encourage him, and enjoy him as a blessing from God]."

Men have a great need to be respected. Don't take him for granted.

"If you treat a man as he is, he will stay as he is. But if you treat him as he were what he ought to be and could be, he will become a bigger and better man" – GEOTHE.

3. A wife's attitude towards financial problems and her husband's attempts to bring in money can either make or break him.

A man can feel like a failure if he's unable to provide for his household (*1 Timothy 5:8*). So don't worsen matters by not supporting him. Be the wise woman that builds her home (*Proverbs 14:1a*). Have purposeful money conversations. *Refer to question 14 on money matters.*

4. Make up your mind to obey God's word, whether you feel like it or not.

If you are struggling with submission to your husband, look inward for deeper unresolved issues. Unburden to the Lord. (*Extract from Oludoyi, G (2015), I Pronounce You*

Husband and Wife!, Revised Edition, London: Baruch Press, 168-171)

"When a woman submits to her husband, it is not because she is afraid of his reprove, domination, rejection or chastisement, instead, it is because she chooses to bless him and by so doing, she is demonstrating a spirit of respect for him. A woman that submits to her husband, including her laid-back husband is a woman with strength of character. When a wife submits to her husband she is simultaneously submitting to the Lord, 'as to the Lord,' serves as a motivation for the wife to submit to her husband." *Oludoyi, G (2015), I Pronounce You Husband and Wife! Revised Edition, London: Baruch Press, 168-171*

She can express her opinions and ideas respectfully without belittling or without disrespectful confrontation. God ordains her to be her husband's helper, not his 'doormat'. She is making a choice not to overtly resist her husband's will. Whenever a woman is instructed in Scripture to submit to her husband, there is a corresponding command for husbands to love and cherish their wives. A man who loves his wife, as Christ loved His Church, will not treat her as an inferior; Christ, the head of the Church did not treat his bride (Church) that way.

God has given husbands a clear mandate to treat their wives with tenderness, respect, support and encouragement. **1 Peter 3:7 (NKJV):** *"Husbands, likewise, dwell with them with understanding, giving honor to the wife, as to the weaker vessel, and as being heirs together of the grace of life, that your prayers may not be hindered."*

A wife does not have to submit to an abusive husband. Christ did not abuse the Church. There is no possible justification for a husband to abuse his wife, whether in overtly physical, verbal, or emotional ways. If you are being abused in your marriage, seek help! Don't suffer in silence! *Please, refer to question 29.*

6

MY HUSBAND DOESN'T LISTEN. WHAT DO I DO?

The common complaint women make about their husbands is that they don't listen. It has been scientifically proven that a woman uses both sides of her brain while a man uses only the left side of the brain while listening.

Men don't listen to their partners for several reasons:

Psychologically, men are usually action-oriented listeners who focus mainly on the current situation and the possible solution to the problem they just had. As a result, they easily switch off if the wife deviates from the topic at hand, perhaps through a detailed narration of the issue (information overload!). Listening to the long discussion can be a chore for men. They find it unnecessary, hence they tune their ears off. A man can concentrate on a woman's talk for a few minutes before he switches off because he doesn't find the conversation interesting, whereas he could talk for hours with his mates discussing cars, politics, sports and other topics of interest.

Another reason men don't listen to their wives is because they fear a verbal attack with constant complaints. Just like women are weary of their husbands not listening, the men are weary of their wives' constant complaints or dissatisfaction about one thing or the other, making the men feel inadequate about not being able to solve their wives' problems. To avoid that, they just don't listen to their wives.

At times, men just don't listen in order to avoid conflict that may arise from a conversation, especially when they know they have done something wrong that has upset the wife, e.g. forgetting to do something he promised. They feel it's safe to act deaf. This can actually frustrate the wife. He may not want to listen to avoid conflict.

If you're used to saying hurtful, intimidating, and disrespectful things to his feelings and beliefs, he will get protective and defensive. If you are manipulative, he will tune out. If you talking style is one of preaching, commanding, lecturing, or questioning, he won't listen. If you are giving him advice, it may not be well received. He may feel intimidated or not comfortable expressing his opposing view, so he tunes out.

Repeatedly bringing up old issues or topics can make him tune out. Your constant complaining, nagging, whining, or speaking negatively can wear him out. Comments that use words like "always, never, constantly" can cause him to ignore you. **Proverbs 21:9 (NKJV):** *"Better to dwell in a corner of a housetop, Than in a house shared with a contentious woman."*

Proverbs 29:19 (NKJV): *"Better to dwell in the wilderness, Than with a contentious and angry woman."*

How you get him to listen:

1. Be clear about your expectations. Men are not mind readers. Be very clear with your problems and what you expect of him. You can even tell him clearly that you need him to only listen , because you feel like venting out your feelings, and it is okay if he does not have solutions.
2. Stick to the important point and don't go into too many details. Provide more details if he asks.
3. Check your body language and the tone of voice. Our nonverbal communications accounts for 55% of the message. Avoid a confrontational posture, and refrain from raising your voice or shouting. These will be counterproductive and will get you nowhere.
4. Choose an appropriate time and place to vent your frustration. Bringing up important issues

when your husband is busy, tired, watching his favourite sport or TV show, or preoccupied with something else will make him not listen to you. Instead, he will remain silent and pretend to be listening. No matter how urgent or tempting the situation is, don't talk about serious topics over the phone when he is at work or busy with something else. Let your effort not be in vain. Rather, choose a time and place where he has no choice but to listen.

5. If possible, let your husband decide when he is ready to talk. Let him know you want to discuss something with him. Let him come up with the best time and place so that he knows you don't want to fight. This will make him approach you with an open mind.

6. Let him know the gravity of what you are saying, especially if he is trivialising your concerns. He may not see things from your own perspective. Let him know about how you and the family will be affected if the issue is not resolved. Let him know you are for peace and progress.

7. Lastly, have a laugh and make fun together. Life is too short to be at constant loggerheads.

7

WHY DOES MY WIFE ALWAYS NAG?

W hat is nagging? – Nagging according to Webster's dictionary, is "to irritate by constant scolding or urging."

It is repetitive inquiring, asking, or reminding, with a tone of escalating irritability to both the nagger and the nagged. This mode of communication is not effective. **Proverbs 27:15 (NKJV):** *"A continual dripping on a very rainy day and a contentious woman are alike;"*

The nagging wife's notion is one of the most common negative stereotypes about married women.

What is behind this stereotype, and why have women been characterized in this way for so long? One argument is that men and women speak two different languages. Consequently, what sounds like a reasonable request from a man translates into an irritating nag from a woman. When a man nags, he is often referred to as being demanding or domineering. A nagging wife might whine or plead, whereas a husband may yell and demand.

Usually, wives will complain that their husbands won't do what they say they will do, they don't complete tasks, therefore, they can't rely on them. This results in feeling disrespected, ignored, unimportant, overburdened, and unloved.

Many women who nag don't even realise they are doing it. They think they're just trying to help. At times, they nag because they're angry or feel that they're not listened to. There is distrust, and intimacy is affected. Walls go up, while the husband feels like they are constantly on the defence or under attack; both parties experience frustrations and irritations.

Constant nagging can make you feel like a parent to your spouse, and he also feels treated like a child which can cause resentment and bitterness towards you. Nagging can also hinder intimacy and trust in the relationship.

A woman's nagging can be a cry for help. Women, as multitaskers, are usually prompt when it comes to carrying out their responsibilities in the home. When a man does not live up to his roles and responsibilities, this can provoke nagging by the wife. Understand her perspective and negotiate with her. You need to understand that your wife is not a superwoman; her nagging at you is a cry for help.

If your wife is always nagging, talk it out. Try to understand why she's nagging you constantly. Choose the right words, tone, time, and attitude. Identify your mistakes and apologise. Listen to what she has to say. Try to see things from her perspective. Talk about your perspective and negotiate with her.

Remember, marriage is about adjustments and compromise, and there is nothing that can't be resolved. Work on yourself and live up to your responsibilities. Talk to a counsellor if things don't improve. This may help deal with pent-up anger and frustration.

8

I DON'T LIKE ARGUING WITH MY HUSBAND, BUT IT HAPPENS A LOT. WHAT CAN I DO TO STOP THIS?

C onflicts are a normal part of any relationship. No matter how much you love each other, you won't see eye to eye on everything. Conflict is inevitable. It is how you deal with it that matters.

James 1:19 (NKJV)*: "So then, my beloved brethren, let every man be swift to hear, slow to speak, slow to wrath."*

Ephesians 4:26 (NKJV)*: "Be angry, and do not sin": do not let the sun go down on your wrath."*

Problems in a marriage are simply any issue or difficulty that needs solving or sorting out.

Conflicts are problems that have become infected. They occur where the problem has brought about a heated argument, a row, or an angry silence. Are you arguing about what you think you're really arguing about, or are there other things going on that worry you? If you are arguing all the time, this will be detrimental to a healthy marriage. Learning ways to handle disagreements constructively is crucial.

Common areas of conflict are:

Money, sex, children, work, housework (chores), in-laws, conflicting personal habits, ill health & ageing.

The main characteristic of conflict is its deadly ability to escalate. Conflicts don't normally appear in an instant.

Many conflicts between couples occur because of any of the following:

- Each has a *different thinking pattern or process* that leads to conflict.
- Each has a *different communication style* that leads to conflict.
- Each has a *lack of understanding and connection* with the other.

In resolving a conflict, the three elements of conflict must be dealt with, i.e., issue, relationship, and emotions .

According to John Gottman, a renowned marriage psychologist, negative interactions are balanced by positive ones in stable marriages.

There is a very specific ration in stable marriages, 5 to 1, between the number of positive feelings and interactions and negative interactions.

In contrast, couples who are likely to divorce, have too little positive interactions to compensate for the rising negativity in their marriages.

According to Gottman, positivity must outweigh negativity 5 to 1, whether couples have intense fights or avoid conflicts completely. There are successful adjustments in these marriages that keep the couples together.

Some examples of positive interactions:

- Showing interest in one another's lives.
- Being affectionate and tender.
- Showing you care by thoughtful acts.
- Expressing your concern and listening.
- Being accepting of a different opinion but respectfully disagreeing when needed.
- Being empathetic through verbal and non-verbal expressions.
- Expressing laughter and joy and sharing these together.

Gottman describes four primary toxic behaviours (destructive forces) that contribute to couples feeling disconnected from each other.

According to him, these four negative patterns are like *the four horsemen of the Apocalypse in the Book of Revelations chapter 6, "they spell the end of days".*

1. Criticism – the most dangerous. Silent love killer. Showing constant disapproval, fault-finding and blames spouse's personality and character. invalidation (constant putting down the spouse's thoughts, feelings, and character).
2. Contempt – intent to insult psychologically, abuse of spouse, name-calling, negative non-verbal actions, e.g. rolling of the eyes, mocking, and character assassination.
3. Defensiveness – a natural protective response to diffuse attacks from the spouse, defensive statements, making excuses, cross-complaining, whining, yes-butting and body language. It obstructs communication, hence escalates conflict.
4. Stonewalling – often happens while a couple is talking. Stony silence, non-responsiveness to the spouse. Used more by husbands than by wives. The silent retreat irritates a wife and sends her the message that he doesn't love her.

As these behaviours increase, loneliness and isolation also increase, and there is a likelihood of marital disintegration that could lead to divorce.

(John Gottman & Nan Silver, 2007) Why Marriages Succeed or Fail And How to Make Yours Last. Bloomsbury Publishing Plc, London W1D 3QY; pages 68-102

Principles of Effective Conflict Resolution:

How can a couple deal effectively with conflict?

I have used the acronym **CONFLICT** to describe some principles of conflict resolution.

Communicate your hurts and negative feelings in a constructive way. There will be times when you will feel bitterness, resentment, disappointment, or disapproval. These feelings need to be communicated for change to occur. How you express these thoughts is critical. Make "I" - "you" - statements, e.g. instead of using accusatory statements such as "you really frustrate me when you pay the bills late", use a more personal approach- "I feel frustrated when the bills are paid late". The "you" statement connotes blame and criticism, whereas the "I" statement invites a dialogue.

Overlook faults. Forgiveness is key. Overcome your desire to revenge.

No name calling, ridicule, insult mindreading or character assassination.

Focus on the issue at hand than attacking each other. Face each other, don't bring up past failures. Limit the conflict to the here and now, and focus on behaviour rather than character.

Listen actively without being defensive to your spouse's opinion , even if you disagree with what is being said. Seek to understand his or her views and ask questions to clarify viewpoints.

Identify the core of the issue. Identifying it is the beginning of the resolution.

Compromise when possible. This is a major part of conflict resolution. Find a middle ground that can allow both of you to feel satisfied with the outcome. Consider all the factors in a conflict before bringing it up with your spouse.

Timely resolution is necessary. Talk to your spouse first before talking with others. If necessary, seek wise counsel to help resolve the issue.

Adapted from (Oludoyi, G 2018) 10 Relationship Commandments. Designxpirit, UK; pages 124 - 125

9

SHOULD A WOMAN ALWAYS BE THE ONE TO LOOK AFTER THE CHILDREN AT HOME WHILE THE HUSBAND WORKS?

The patriarchal norm of males being the breadwinner and females the housewives in times past is no more prevalent today. Family life is changing, and so too is the role mothers and fathers play at work and home. Many two-parent households have both parents working full-time to make ends meet. The decision to be a stay-at-home mum and a working dad is one that each couple must make.

The key to making a marriage successful when one parent is a stay-at-home mum and father goes to work, is effective communication between the couple. Both the mother's caregiver role and the father's provider role are vital. Neither role is superior to or inferior to the other. They are equally important roles that should be seen as partnership, where each spouse respects the other. Husbands need their wives to understand the pressure they're under to provide for the family and how isolated from their children they feel.

Some husbands fail to understand how complicated, and conflicted women's feelings might be about being home alone all day with the children. The stay-at-home mum can feel lonely, overwhelmed, stressed, burnt out, depressed, sad, and angry. She may feel intellectually under-stimulated, and this can cause resentment. Empathy and appreciation are vital. The stay-at-home mum- likewise needs to understand the pressure and stresses the man may sometimes be dealing with as the breadwinner. Work can be intellectually challenging and exhausting, and stay-at-home work can be physically challenging and exhausting as well.

Lack of sleep, lack of free time, and tiredness can make couples get mad at each other. Therefore patience, empathy, appreciation, and forgiveness are crucial. The couple should work on their relationship and not put it on the back burner. Their sexual intimacy should not be compromised. Connecting with each other daily makes a huge difference.

Deciding to stay at home or go to work is one of the biggest and most challenging decisions a mother will make and it shouldn't be criticised. Every mother makes that decision based on what she feels is best for the family. and that decision should be accepted and respected.

A husband should make it part of his marriage routine to check in about the day-to-day details, joys and frustrations. He should make it a priority to at least add one household or parenting task to his routine. He should offer to help. He should also make an effort to be actively involved in the children's lives.

It is necessary for the stay-at-home mum to establish a support network outside the home. Meeting up with other mum friends can reduce stress and prevent burnout. There are lots of online opportunities and business for personal development. Consider starting a new hobby. These little things will make a huge difference in your mental wellbeing and functioning.

If the couple involved feel like a team working together to give the family the best life possible, the marriage would be wholesome. **Ecclesiastes 4:9 (NKJV):** *"Two are better than one, because they have a good reward for their labor."*

10

I EARN MORE THAN MY HUSBAND. I CAN TELL IT IS CAUSING HIM TO RESENT ME. THERE IS TENSION IN OUR MARRIAGE THAT WASN'T THERE BEFORE. WHAT DO I DO?

Resentment from your husband is not unusual in men who have breadwinner wives. A man whose wife earns more than him has lost the classic gender role of the breadwinner in the home. His work and earning are linked to his self-esteem, identity and sense of achievement. A man prides himself on autonomy, power, and competence. They feel empowered when needed, e.g. as providers. Hence, if financially he is not needed, he may feel less than a man. **1 Timothy 5:8 (NKJV):** *"But if anyone does not provide for his own, and especially for those of his household, he has denied the faith and is worse than an unbeliever."* A man's ego may not fare so well when their wives earn more. Your husband's resentment is likely masking underlying insecurity (this, however, is not true of all men, just some). It is easier for him to turn to anger than to experience vulnerability; hence, the resentment and tension. This situation is obviously unhealthy for your marriage.

What do you do?

Have a candid discussion with your husband. Choose the right time to have this discussion. There is no greater loss than the right advice given at the wrong time. Start by telling him how you feel. Avoid criticism, blaming, shouting, insults, or confrontation since your aim is not to worsen things but rather come to a good resolution. **Proverbs 15:1-8 (NKJV):** *"A soft answer turns away wrath, but a harsh word stirs up anger.*

The tongue of the wise uses knowledge rightly, but the mouth of fools pours forth foolishness.

The eyes of the Lord are in every place, keeping watch on the evil and the good.

A wholesome tongue is a tree of life, but perverseness in it breaks the spirit.

A fool despises his father's instruction, but he who receives correction is prudent.

In the house of the righteous there is much treasure, but in the revenue of the wicked is trouble.

The lips of the wise disperse knowledge, but the heart of the fool does not do so.

The sacrifice of the wicked is an abomination to the Lord, but the prayer of the upright is His delight."

Show some appreciation and gratitude for his own input into the family and his unwavering support (if that is so). He may get defensive, and unconsciously project his resentment and anger on you. Remind him that you are a team and not in competition with each other. Let him clarify expectations of each other. Have money conversations if necessary.

Don't apologise or downplay your success. If not, you could in turn become resentful towards him. Two wrongs can't make a right. Your success should be his success; your win, his win. After all you are both in this together. **Ecclesiastes 4:9 (NKJV):** *"Two are better than one, because they have a good reward for their labor."*

If you are the sole breadwinner and your husband is the stay-at-home partner, don't take each other for granted. Praise is crucial on both sides. Men want respect, and women want to feel cherished. Sexual intimacy is important. If your husband feels emasculated and insecure about his role, you need to let him know that you still desire him and, that he is still your man. If sex disappears, or you reject his advances, he is going to feel more hurt and resentful.

Remember you are a team! **Amos 3:3 (NKJV):** *"Can two walk together, unless they are agreed?"*

11

WHAT SHOULD I DO IF MY MOTHER-IN-LAW IS UNDERMINING ME? HOW DO I GET MY HUSBAND TO ADDRESS IT?

Genesis 2:24 (NKJV): *"Therefore a man shall leave his father and mother and be joined to his wife, and they shall become one flesh."*

Your in-laws are a crucial part of your spouse's life; hence they are a crucial part of your life as well. When a man leaves his parents to cleave to his wife; it involves a geographical and psychological breaking away from his original parental ties. Leaving doesn't mean abandoning your parents and no longer showing interest in them; it means the couple sever the tie of dependency and allegiance and establish a new authority for themselves. After marriage, your priority and loyalty must be towards your spouse and your parents should take note of this!

Problems with in-laws is an age-old challenge. In general, women may be more likely to be negatively affected by in-laws than men. Some research psychologists claim that most of the in-law problems are predominantly feminine and this mainly stems from the husband's mother. This may be due to the mother and son bond right from childhood. Sadly, some husbands have not yet severed the "umbilical cord" with their mothers. A man who puts his mother first before his wife will not have a wholesome marriage. Common complaints tend to originate from the daughter in law citing various problems such as the mother-in-law being pushy or having too much influence on the husband. Sometimes it can also be a question of the mother-in-law being disrespectful to the daughter in law, which can be perceived as crossing marital boundaries. This seems to be the case in your own marriage.

What should you do?

Firstly, discuss your feelings with your husband. He is the principal person to resolve the problem. Let him know how his mother is undermining you. It may be difficult for him to see things that way, probably because that is how his mother has always been. I am sure he wants harmony and peace both in his marriage and with his family. Don't nag, shout, or threw a tantrum about it. Don't put him in a situation where he must choose between you and his mother. It may be hard for him to adjust his focus to create harmony in the marriage.

Show love and kindness towards your mother-in-law. Look for ways to enhance and improve your relationship with his mother and his entire family. You may have to make some healthy compromises. Forgive her and pray for her. Be patient and exercise the fruit of the Spirit. I know this may not be easy but doing this pays off in the end. **Exodus 20:12 (NKJV):** *"Honour your father and your mother, that your days may be long upon the land which the LORD your God is giving you."*

Let your husband firmly draw the necessary boundaries of communication and interaction with your in-laws (his family). Let him make them understand that his allegiance is now to you, with no disrespect to them. This may not be easy for him as he may not be emotionally and spiritually equipped to change without outside help and your patience, support, encouragement, and prayers.

Also ensure that your own family honour your marriage and have regard for your husband. It works both ways.

In the end, if there is a mutually thriving relationship with both families, it becomes a win-win situation for everyone. You will not just benefit from your family and in-laws, but your children will also gain from interactions with their grandparents and even great grandparents. They have a lot to offer them - words of wisdom, stories of old, sharing of life experiences, gifts etc.

12

IS IT ALRIGHT FOR THE HUSBAND TO CONTINUE HANGING OUT WITH HIS FRIENDS AND GO ON MEN'S OUTINGS AS IF THEY'RE STILL SINGLE?

Friends are a vital part of our life. The support and advice will guide you through good and bad times.

Proverbs 17:17 (NKJV): *"A friend loves at all times, And a brother is born for adversity."*

However, they can destroy a marital relationship. Sometimes they find it hard to let their married friends spend most of their time with their spouses. They begin to interfere with the marriage.

Some friends expect a newly married friend to continue to be as committed to hanging out and doing things together as he or she had previously been. They feel let down when their friend declines to go out for whatever reason; and they may begin to resent him or her for getting married in the first place. At times, they are resentful towards a spouse for taking away their friend. In such cases, the married person has to stand up to the friends.

The wife or husband is the priority now. Boundaries should be set right from the start of the marriage.

Be open and sensitive to your spouse's need for friends. He may not be trying to get away from you if he spends a lot of time with friends. He may be trying to prove to himself that he can balance all of his relationships. Ultimately, discuss the matter together and come up with a solution as a couple. Refrain from speaking badly of your husband's friends.

Hopefully, with a good talk, you and your spouse can come up with an arrangement that honours your time together and respects time spent apart.

13

IS THIS OKAY FOR A HUSBAND OR WIFE TO BE COMMUNICATING WITH HIS OR HER EX-WITH OR WITHOUT THE KNOWLEDGE OF THE OTHER?

A secure and trusting romantic relationship rests upon a foundation of trust, honesty and transparency. This trust cannot be established if either one of the partners remains in contact with a former lover. If a spouse chooses to communicate with an ex-girlfriend or ex-boyfriend, especially without the knowledge of the spouse, trust is compromised in the marriage. Trust breached is hard to restore. **Proverbs 11:3 (NKJV):** *"The integrity of the upright will guide them, But the perversity of the unfaithful will destroy them."*

If a husband and wife deem it fit to rekindle communication with their ex, it is necessary to keep the other spouse in the know. If your conversations and interactions with your ex are innocent and purposeful, I don't see why that should be done in secret without your spouse knowing. Secrecy can breed lies, deception, distraction, rekindling of old burning desires towards each other, and even an affair. **Colossians 3:9 (NKJV):** *"Do not lie to one another, since you have put off the old man with his deeds,"*

If you honour your marriage and love and respect your spouse, why do you want to threaten your marriage?

There is nothing hidden under the sun, even under your own roof.

Luke 8:17 (NKJV): *"For nothing is secret that will not be revealed, nor anything hidden that will not be known and come to light."*

What you are doing secretly will sooner or later be known to your spouse. It will not just arouse jealousy, but will cause fights, conflicts and may even lead to marital breakdown. If there are issues in your marriage, instead of contacting your ex for solace or to unburden why not seek help from others such as counsellors or pastors to resolve the issue? Give no place to the enemy!

Proverbs 6:27-28 (NKJV): *"Can a man take fire to his bosom, and his clothes not be burned?*

Can one walk on hot coals, and his feet not be seared?"

Luke 7:21 (NKJV): *"And that very hour He cured many of infirmities, afflictions, and evil spirits; and to many blind He gave sight."*

If your spouse has an ex-wife or ex-husband, it is crucial you and your spouse discuss your rules of engagement with your ex, especially if children are involved. Talk about your ex's role in your spouse and children's life and then discuss your spouse relationship with the ex.

If you need to discuss with your ex perhaps about the children, your husband or wife should be aware. Instead of getting upset over your spouse calling his or her ex without telling you, calm down and at a suitable time, discuss it with your husband/wife.

If he or she understands how you feel, they may be more open to respecting you and your feelings.

However, if you flare up, he or she may try to hide their behaviour to avoid confrontation with you and continue this habit.

You must make it clear to him or her that communications with their ex without your knowledge is not acceptable and your first loyalties are to each other.

If it is about his or her children, you can work together to ensure the children get to see their dad or mum and that your spouse is not manipulated by their ex.

Transparency and honesty are paramount!

14

WHY DO WE KEEP FIGHTING OVER MONEY ISSUES?

Ecclesiastes 7:12a (NKJV): *"for wisdom is a defense as money is a defense,....."*

Ecclesiastes 10:19b (KJV): *"... money answereth all things."*

The number one issue that couples fight about is money. Money issues don't discriminate. They affect both marriages of the wealthy and the poor.

Money in marriage is not just about numbers. Money represents emotions, beliefs and behaviours, which are all very personal. Money touches every decision you make.

Each spouse has different histories and has learned different habits associated with money, and when they come together, there is a potential for tension.

There are more than 800 verses in the Bible about finances and for a good reason. How we handle money is a good indicator of who we are and what we believe. It is one way to test our faith and, to see whether we are willing to trust God.

It doesn't make any difference whether or not a couple has money. Suppose the couple has different spending habits, different saving goals, different thoughts about investing, and different fears about being poor (this is usually why God often brings opposites together in marriage. A spender is often attracted to a saver or vice versa), then financial conflicts will eventually surface in the marriage.

According to the Money couple, Scott and Bethany Palmer, there are five money personalities: the Saver, the Spender, the Risk-taker, the Security-seeker and the Flyer. Take their Money Personality Assessment to find out your money personality on *www.themoneycouple.com*

Financial problems are a leading cause of divorce. Lack of communication is the source of many marital problems. Financial anxieties if not addressed, can become bigger problems with much more difficult solutions.

Partners should fully disclose their assets, liabilities, and credit reports to each other before marriage. Disclose responsibilities you have for members of your family. Obtain both your credit reports and scores and financial responsibilities for children from a previous relationship. The spouse should not be in the dark about their spouse's finances.

At times, some spouses don't know what accounts exist, what bills need to be paid, or what the passwords are to log in to each account. What if one spouse dies suddenly or is too sick to handle the financial tasks?

A couple's financial literacy should include: personal financial planning, creating a budget, setting goals, managing debts and discretionary spending.

There is no one-size fits all for dealing with marriage problems because not all types of conflicts are alike.

Common money issues:

1. What's mine, yours and ours?
2. Debt – school loan, car loan, credit cards, gambling habits, financial baggage, debts incurred before marriage.
3. Opposing attitudes towards money (spender or saver). Money personality differences.
4. Powerplay, e.g. if a spouse has a paid job and the other has no job, both spouses would like to be working, but one is unemployed; one spouse earns more than the other; one spouse comes from a wealthy home and the other doesn't. When these situations are present, the money earner (or the one who earns more) often wants

to dictate the couple's spending priorities, but both spouses need to cooperate as a team.

5. Expenses associated with children.
6. Extended family expenses.
7. Mismatched money priorities.
8. Financial infidelity, e.g. secret accounts, undisclosed debts, gambling addictions, hidden buys, overbudgeting, expensive buys, impulsive buys, joint accounts peculiarities.
9. Unexpected major expenses, e.g. major house repairs, unplanned trips etc.
10. Poor money management skills. Proper money management discussed before 'I do' is crucial.

One of the financial decisions that each couple must make involves their level of financial commitment to God and the Church.

The biblical method of stewardship is tithing and offerings. As a couple, you must establish God's word as the final authority in all financial matters in your home. Let it influence your decisions on spending, saving, giving, investing, allowances and other related issues you need to make over time.

How to handle money issues:

- Communication and honesty in conveying expectations, hopes, goals and anxieties. Money is one of the most difficult topics for couples.

No matter how uncomfortable it feels, the two most important words to remember about marriage and money are: never lie. Honesty is crucial. Lying about finances to a spouse damages trust and can lead to divorce. **Proverbs 26:28 (NKJV):** *"A lying tongue hates those who are crushed by it, And a flattering mouth works ruin."*

- Deal with debts.
- Discover your money personality. (Are you a spender, risk-taker, flyer, saver, or security-seeker?)
- Check your ego. The power-play issue can stir up arguments quickly. Few things build resentment faster than being made to feel inferior. If you've got the money, you need to be sensitive about how you present spending discussions. If you don't have the money, you need to be prepared for the stress and tension that are almost inevitable. Studies have shown that people with more power are more likely to act selfishly, impulsively, aggressively, and approach others with less empathy.
- While joint accounts offer greater transparency and access, it is not in itself a solution to an unbalanced power – money dynamics in marriage.
- Address family matters. Extended family can be a huge challenge and no single piece of advice

will properly address every situation and the emotions inevitably attached to them. Living with a resentful, angry and frustrated spouse can be a miserable experience. Having a policy agreed upon in advance, e.g. asking for consent can help prevent trouble.

- Passing on good money habits to your children. Use allowances and goals to teach them about earning, saving and spending money.
- The best way to be sure you and your spouse are on the same page with your finances is to talk about them regularly, honestly, and without judgement. Don't do it when you're angry or tired. Schedule times either once a month or quarterly, or annually to check-in on short-term and long-term financial goals.
- Consider seeing a financial adviser.
- Beware of 'lifestyle inflation', which means making more money, which brings about a corresponding increase in spending. All to keep up with the Joneses.
- Consistently look for ways to improve your finances. And remember, as a couple, your view toward money should be: "our money is yours, mine, and ours."

15

SHOULD CHRISTIAN COUPLES HAVE PRENUPS?

A pre-nuptial agreement is an agreed-on contract created before marriage that indicates how money and possessions will be divided if the couple divorces.

Lawyers advocate for prenups because of the era of high divorce rates.

Prenups are typically recommended for two reasons:

1. Wealth protection. When one person brings a lot of wealth into the marriage, and the other does not, or when one stands to receive a sizeable inheritance.

2. Other person protection. There are situations where your marriage may impact other people financially e.g. children from a previous marriage.

For a believer, marriage is a lifelong covenant relationship between husband and wife, with vows exchanged, enduring through hard times, financial crisis, trials, etc., for better, for worse, for richer, for poorer, till death do us part.

Genesis 2:24 (NKJV): *"Therefore a man shall leave his father and mother and be joined to his wife, and they shall become one flesh."*

From a biblical viewpoint, marriage is a hundred percent commitment.

The psychology of prenuptial agreements encourages each spouse to think of herself or himself as separate from the other, to be suspicious of the other, and to hold on tightly to what's yours and keep it from the other. The existence of a prenup sets the husband and wife at odds with each other. It undermines the relationship, putting the sacred covenant on shaky ground from the beginning. Prenup communicates:

1. Distrust in the relationship can cause hurt. Prenup is like a protective mechanism.
2. Uncertainty about the longevity of the marriage. Will it last?
3. "Yours", "mine", "ours" mindset.

Proverbs 31:11 (KJV): *"The heart of her husband doth safely trust in her, so that he shall have no need of spoil."*

If believers are considering a prenup, it is worthwhile to ask the motive for the prenup.

There may be instances where a prenup is justified. For instance, a blended family and inheritance or trust funds for children from a previous marriage, significant debt incurred before marriage, or a business created before marriage. Other possible reasons people request prenups are fear of being taken advantage of, negative experiences with money or lack of financial security, residual hurt, pain or anger from a previous marriage, and a desire for control and selfishness.

If your fiancé is requesting it, there need to be deep conversations regarding it. Talk about money, family history, childhood experiences, financial training, spending habits, financial goals, and money personalities.

Seek counsel from a Christian counsellor.

16

IS IT GOOD FOR A MAN TO HIDE IMPORTANT INFORMATION ABOUT HIS HEALTH, WORK AND PROPERTY FROM HIS WIFE AND CHILDREN?

No, it is not good!

Trust is the central ingredient to a lasting marriage. Without it, marriages don't work. Hiding things in a marriage is never wise. Being secretive and hiding things from one another will only cause pain in the long run and make a marriage far more hard work than it need to be.

I totally agree with the statement by Dave Willis, host for the TV show *Marriage Today*.

"In marriage, secrets are as dangerous as lies. Marriage *must* be built on a foundation of total transparency and trust. You must prioritize trust and transparency in the marriage ahead of your own personal privacy. Unless you're planning a surprise party or hiding a holiday gift, there are no places for secrets in marriage. Anytime you're having a conversation, making a purchase, sending a text message, doing an internet search or doing anything else you hope your spouse never finds out about, your secrecy is actually an act of infidelity." (*Dave Willis*)

www.marriagemissions.com/privacy-vs-secrecy-marriage

What do men commonly hide from their wives - their finances, interactions with women, when they are hurting or undergoing stress, sexual dissatisfaction, illness and more.

Keeping secrets from one another undermines the authenticity of the marriage. These secrets are actions, beliefs or parts of ourselves that we deliberately keep hidden out of fear of their impact. Fear of a spouse's reaction can cause men to begin to hide something. However, there is nothing hidden that will not be disclosed.

Luke 8:17 (NKJV): *"For nothing is secret that will not be revealed, nor anything hidden that will not be known and come to light."*

Having affairs, secret bank accounts, investments, properties, and secrets of this nature erode trust and security. It also creates a chasm that makes it difficult for a couple to feel close and truly connected. These secrets, over time, get discovered and could have disastrous consequences. A husband holding secrets creates a false persona and lives a 'double life'. This creates feelings of betrayal, vulnerability and insecurity in the wife.

Proverbs 28:13 (NKJV): *"He who covers his sins will not prosper, but whoever confesses and forsakes them will have mercy."*

Protective buffering, i.e., information hiding in a relationship, has its disadvantages. By keeping information or, a secret, thinking you are trying to protect your spouse by hiding information from them that you perceive as harmful. Though the aim of hiding information is to help the spouse cope by making his or her worry less; however, this can harm the relationship. When your spouse does eventually find out (which usually happens), it may strain the relationship.

Some men hide health-related information to shield the wife from the stress that comes with knowing about a diagnosis or symptoms, e.g. cancer diagnosis. Perhaps to keep the wife from stressing or burdening her with bad news, the man thinks he can handle it all alone. He wants to project that he has it all together. Keeping such important information from your spouse can be harmful to your mental and physical health. This leads to serious stress for the man as his wife cannot offer the much-needed support at such a time.

Secrecy leads to lies and being dishonest. The question is, is it more harmful to reveal the secret or is it more harmful to conceal the secret? Secrets cause disconnection. Spouses can intuitively sense when there is a distance, no matter the degree.

Many men are afraid to stress, for the same reasons they don't share hurt. They want to project that they have it all together. The other reason is that they think the wife can't handle it. Women are perceptive, and most likely already know. By not letting her know, you are forcing her to use her imagination to figure out what's wrong. This can hurt her and the marriage. Invite your wife into your stress. Sharing your insecurities and fears will make you close.

Proverbs 31:11-12 (NKJV): *"The heart of her husband safely trusts her; So he will have no lack of gain.*

She does him good and not evil All the days of her life."

Remember, secrets, big or small, erode trust. Trust once broken takes years to repair.

17

I DON'T ENJOY SEX WITH MY HUSBAND, AND I DON'T KNOW WHY. CAN YOU HELP ME?

G reat sex makes life enjoyable. It is a panacea of life's little woes. Work hassles, financial worries, problem with children, or in-laws seem much more manageable when sex is wonderful. On the other hand, lousy sex (or no sex) can make life seem like a drudge. If sex isn't great, women struggle to enjoy sex. It is a common issue and a complicated one because the reasons for these feeling can vary widely from one woman to another.

It could be a physical problem or psychological or both, and it can hamper a relationship as the couple feel isolated and less connected.

Female sexual dysfunction can be in five categories:

- Low libido
- Painful sex

- Difficulty being aroused
- Aversion to sex
- Inability to achieve orgasm

Most women need clitoral stimulation with fingers to reach orgasm during sex.

If you find in-and-out penetration not that enjoyable, ask your spouse to refocus their attention on your clitoris during sex.

History of sexual trauma e.g. child abuse, sexual assault, may hinder enjoying sex. Some cope by disassociating themselves from the sexual act; hence, lack of engagement and pleasure.

The shame surrounding sex and other emotions like fear, guilt, embarrassment about having sex can make it hard to relax; hence making arousal difficult and may cause pain. Poor body image and low self-esteem can impact one's ability to enjoy sex.

Female genital mutilation (FGM) can present with a range of symptoms including lack of libido, arousability and orgasm. Psychological support, physiotherapy and on occasion, reconstructive surgery are some measures in treating sexual dysfunction in FGM sufferers.

Childbirth or looking after children with an overload of chores can also put a woman off sex.

See your doctor, who may offer some helpful advice or refer you to a specialist for an assessment and treatment.

Men see sex as a pure pleasure disconnected from emotional commitment. Most women need to feel physical and emotional closeness and tenderness before wanting to have sex. Making love confirms intimacy rather than creates it for a woman. A common sexual turnoff for women is that men want to have sex even if they feel distant, argumentative, or angry. Such differences can make a woman pull away from sexual expression.

Low sex drive (low libido) can be caused by illness, medication, contraceptive pills, antidepressants, stress, and post-child-birth.

Pain during sex is a common problem that affects three out of four women in their lifetime. This can be caused by vulvodynia (a pain disorder that affects the vulva), sexually transmitted diseases (STDs) such as chlamydia, herpes, hormonal changes during perimenopause and menopause caused by decreasing levels of estrogen leading to causing vaginal dryness.

Gynaecological conditions such as pelvic inflammatory disease, endometriosis, fibroids, inflammatory bowel disease etc., can also cause painful sex.

Vaginismus is an involuntary contraction of muscles around the opening of the vagina which causes pain.

Treatment of painful sex:

Use lubricants, make time for sex, talk to your spouse, try sexual activities that don't cause pain, take painkillers, and take it to God in prayer. If it persists, seek medical advice.

There are very few things that cannot be worked on in a marriage or even repaired and resolved.

18

MY HUSBAND WANTS ORAL SEX, BUT I AM NOT SURE IF IT'S PERMITTED BEFORE GOD. I WANT TO PLEASE MY HUSBAND; WHAT DO I DO?

The Bible does not directly address the issue of oral sex.

I believe what happens behind closed doors, in the bedroom is between the couple. They are to decide for themselves what they want.

Many believers do not approve of this form of sex.

What is oral sex? In oral sex, the woman receives the penis into her mouth to stimulate the glans of the penis with her lips and tongue (*fellatio*). Likewise, the man can stimulate the clitoris of the woman with his tongue (*cunnilingus*). These sexual acts, if prolonged, can bring an orgasm. Some couples use these acts as a form of foreplay before the actual sexual intercourse.

The Biblical sexual ethics is to consider your spouse, before yourself.

1 Corinthians 7:3-5 (NKJV): *"Let the husband render to his wife the affection due her, and likewise also the wife to her husband. The wife does not have authority over her own body, but the husband does. And likewise the husband does not have authority over his own body, but the wife does. Do not deprive one another except with consent for a time, that you may give yourselves to fasting and prayer; and come together again so that Satan does not tempt you because of your lack of self-control".*

Examine your intention. Is it really a loving act for you and your spouse?

Are you engaging in oral sex as a way to enjoy your spouse or are your actions used to dominate or control him or her? Is your spouse a willing partner to this?

1 Peter 3:7 (NET): *"Husbands, in the same way, treat your wives with consideration as the weaker partners and show them honor as fellow heirs of the grace of life. In this way nothing will hinder your prayers".* This consideration includes what satisfies and stimulates her and what is offensive.

Neither spouse should be forced or coerced into doing something he or she is not completely comfortable with. If you have to pressure your spouse for oral sex, despite he or she being opposed to it, or against their conscience, then think otherwise. Having your way against his or her wish makes you unkind, self-centered, and inconsiderate.

I might as well talk about anal sex.

Anal sex is the introduction of the penis into the anus of the woman. The normal function of the anus is a passage for faeces and not to receive the penis. Anal sex is considered, therefore, unnatural use of that part of the body. *"And likewise also the men , leaving the natural use of the woman..."* **Romans 1:27 (NKJV).**

Therefore, it is not recommended.

19

CAN ONE HAVE SEX WHILE FASTING?

There are about seven reasons God created sex: for procreation, pleasure, protection, peacemaking, proximity, problem solving and powerful release of tension (relaxant). God wants married couples to have healthy, enjoyable, and satisfying sexual relations regularly.

Fasting is a time to abstain from all or some kinds of food or drink, especially as a religious observance. It is usually accompanied by prayers and worship. It is a form of spiritual discipline which helps grow one's faith and enhance intimacy with God. There are types of fasts- regular fast, partial fast, liquid fast, and, absolute fast. Fasts vary in duration like half day fast, 24 hours fast, intermittent fast, three days, seven days, 21 days, 40 days fast, and longer.

Sex is such a pleasurable activity, which could get in the way of concentrating on your fast; hence, couples are advised to abstain from sex during the period. However, having sex with your spouse whilst fasting does not make you unclean or unholy.

The question of whether to have sex during fasting periods or not is commonly asked.

If you decide to abstain from sex during fasting, you must both decide to do so for a definite period, according to **1 Corinthians 7:5 (NKJV):** which says, *"Do not deprive one another except with consent for a time, that you may give yourselves to fasting and prayer; and come together again so that Satan does not tempt you because of your lack of self-control".*

A couple must agree on how their sex life will be, especially during a long fast. A lack of clarity on this matter causes discord between married couples, especially in cases where husband and wife have different opinions about what should be done.

So, should Christians have sex while fasting? Abstaining from sex during fasting must be decided by the couple.

20

CAN I HAVE SEX DURING MY PERIODS?

I n answering this question, firstly, let's examine the medical point of view.

From a medical point of view, there are some health risks associated with sexual intercourse during periods:

1. Risk factor for HIV transmission, sexually transmitted diseases (STDs), pelvic inflammatory diseases (PID), some of which can lead to infertility. The transmission of STDs during periods is facilitated by loss of the protective barrier (cervical mucus plug), the presence of iron in the menstrual fluid, the dilated cervical opening, the elevated alkaline PH of the vagina, and the premenstrual peak of oestrogen and progesterone.

2. Increased blood flow because the uterine veins are congested and prone to rupture and damage. Some

women notice that their periods stop one to two days after sexual intercourse because sexual intercourse causes contractions in the uterus resulting in heavier bleeds that discharge more quickly and shorten the period's duration. The period stops faster than usual.

3. Small risk of pregnancy. This is because sperm can survive within the woman's body for three to five days, and in the case of premature ovulation (e.g. a short menstrual cycle of 21-24 days can cause pregnancy).

4. Risk of development of endometriosis.

5. Sex during periods can affect a man's libido and make him temporarily impotent because of the presence and smell of menstrual material.

The psychological state of a woman before periods such as premenstrual syndrome (PMS) and during periods, e.g., painful cramps, anxiety, depression, migraines, low blood pressure, and a low temperature, doesn't favour their mood for sex.

For some, menstruation could be a turn on. On day one oestrogen and testosterone are low, but they start to rise by day three, making them more aroused and sensitive. In some cases, orgasm can relieve menstrual cramps and PMS.

Based on the possible health risks, some doctors don't recommend having sex during periods.

Now, let's explore what the scriptures say about sex during periods.

The Bible gives us three kinds of laws: moral, ceremonial, and judicial.

In the Old Testament law, many ceremonial laws seem very strange to us. For example, there are laws of uncleanness that prohibit touching a corpse, declare uncleanness in birth, sexual intercourse, menstruation, and semen discharge. These are ritual states of uncleanness, not moral uncleanness. These things are not evil in themselves, but they were matters of ceremonial uncleanness.

It is crucial that we know how to interpret ceremonial laws.

Let's look at the central text that addresses menstruation.

Leviticus 15:19-24 (NKJV): *"If a woman has a discharge, and the discharge from her body is blood, she shall be set apart seven days; and whoever touches her shall be unclean until evening.*

Everything that she lies on during her impurity shall be unclean; also everything that she sits on shall be unclean.

Whoever touches her bed shall wash his clothes and bathe in water, and be unclean until evening.

And whoever touches anything that she sat on shall wash his clothes and bathe in water, and be unclean until evening. If anything is on her bed or on anything on which she sits, when he touches it, he shall be unclean until evening.

And if any man lies with her at all, so that her impurity is on him, he shall be unclean seven days; and every bed on which he lies shall be unclean."

The Levitical ceremonial laws, including this one, don't apply today. Christians today are not under the Old Testament ceremonial laws. Jesus' blood sacrifice paid the penalty for sins once and for all.

Romans 10:4 (NKJV): *"For Christ is the end of the law for righteousness to everyone who believes."*

Galatians 3:24-26 (NKJV): *"Therefore the law was our tutor to bring us to Christ, that we might be justified by faith.*

But after faith has come, we are no longer under a tutor.

For you are all sons of God through faith in Christ Jesus."

Ephesians 2:15 (NKJV): *"Having abolished in His flesh the enmity, that is, the law of commandments contained in ordinances, so as to create in Himself one new man from the two, thus making peace."*

From a biblical perspective, today, there is no reason why a married couple cannot have sex during the wife's periods if they both choose to. Though they don't apply today, these ceremonial laws may still matter to some couples and not to others.

Therefore, my opinion is that a husband and wife should agree together about this matter and be mutually comfortable with the decision.

I SECRETLY MASTURBATE TO RELEASE TENSION. I DON'T WANT TO COMMIT FORNICATION. AM I SINNING?

Masturbation is a grey area of sex as the Bible does not explicitly mention it. This is an important topic since masturbation is practised by many men and women, both married and singles.

Masturbation is the self-stimulation of the genitals to achieve arousal and pleasure, usually to the point of orgasm. It is commonly done by touching, stroking, or massaging the penis or clitoris. Some women use sex toys like vibrators to stimulate their vagina.

People masturbate for different reasons – it helps them relax; it makes them feel good; they want to understand their body better; they want to release sexual tension, or their partner isn't around or available. Some Christians believe that masturbation is an act that prevents fornication.

Although these reasons seem logical, let's see what is involved in the act of masturbation:

1. Masturbation is usually accompanied by lustful thoughts. Jesus condemns this (**Matthew 5:28 {NKJV}**: *"But I say to you that whoever looks at a woman to lust for her has already committed adultery with her in his heart."*), (**1 Thessalonians 4:3-5 NKJV**): *"For this is the will of God, your sanctification: that you should abstain from sexual immorality; that each of you should know how to possess his own vessel in sanctification and honor, not in passion of lust, like the Gentiles who do not know God;"*). You hurt yourself because it fixates your mind on unhealthy sexual expressions. Most likely, it is your mind that brings you to the point of masturbation, either with the help of pornography or your own fantasies. Once your mind entertains impure thoughts, impure acts follow.

2. Self-centeredness and distortion of sex. When masturbating you are not having sex or thinking of sex the way it was created to be. It focuses on the physical aspect of sex, ignoring the emotional and spiritual bonding entirely. If you train yourself to experience sex for selfish physical pleasure only, you will be unable to give yourself emotionally and spiritually to

your spouse during sexual intimacy, because you see it as just a physical thing. You will miss out on the true meaning and experience of sex as intended by God. God created sex as a gift to be shared in the one-flesh relationship between a man and a woman *(Genesis 2:24)*.

3. Masturbation, like any appetite-fulfilling activity, can quickly lead to addiction. It is difficult for most people to stop masturbating, even when they marry.

4. Masturbation can lead to shame, guilt, low self-esteem and fear of being found out.

To further convince you that masturbation is better avoided, ask yourself the following questions:

1. Why am I masturbating? *Galatians 5:16-17.*
2. Does it glorify God? *1 Corinthians 10:31.*
3. Do I harbour impure thoughts during the act of masturbating?
4. Am I alienating my spouse (if married) from this experience?
5. Am I expressing the fruit of the Spirit like self-control and temperance? *Galatians 5:22.*
6. Am I opening doors to the enemy into my life through this?

In answering these questions, be fully persuaded.

Couples apart should be cautious about phone sex (i.e. masturbating together) as it could open doors to masturbation alone, lustful fantasies, and pornography.

22

I AM ADDICTED TO PORNOGRAPHY. HOW CAN I STOP IT?

P ornography is a life-controlling addiction, which doesn't just affect one's daily functioning but also impacts one's relationship with God. It can prove tough to overcome. While many other addictions are introduced from outside the body, porn addiction occurs inside the mind and brain limbic system.

Not only does it cause guilt, fear, shame, lies, and betrayal of trust, it can rob you of time, inner peace, emotional intimacy, purity, and a solid fellowship with God.

There are several types of triggers:

A. Situational: environments that create a trigger because of past thoughts or behaviour (like being in the same room or at a certain time of day).

B. Stress/anxiety/loneliness/traumatic events: difficult emotions or situations that trigger you to turn to pornography as a way to escape and deal with these feelings.

C. Visual: innocent exposure to something not pornographic but triggering via social media, movies, photos, etc.

How can you stop it?

1. Admit you are addicted and need help.

2. Avoid triggers and be watchful when you are most vulnerable, e.g. when hungry, angry, lonely, or tired.

3. Put measures in place to minimise the opportunity of viewing e.g. place your computer in a room where everyone can see it, install password protected internet filters, avoid places or situations that you know will lead you to temptation.

4. Get rid of pornographic materials in your possession.

5. Admit the habit to someone. Confide in them - a trusted friend, a pastor, and share your struggles with them. **James 5:16 (NKJV):** *"Confess your trespasses to one another, and pray for one another, that you may be healed. The effective, fervent prayer of a righteous man avails much."* Don't let shame and guilt make you suffer in silence. The power of sin is in secrecy. Have an accountability

partner who can keep you in check, and you can call upon when tempted.

6. Pray fervently and continually. Meditate on the word of God, memorise scriptures that can be invaluable in times of temptation, e.g. *Psalm 119:11; Romans 13:14; 1 Corinthians 6:18.* Don't be too confident in yourself. *1 Corinthians 10:12,13.*

7. Be part of a support group. There are many sufferers on a recovery journey too. You are not alone.

8. Even if you lapse, get up again. Be patient with yourself and remember your successes. Give yourself grace to fail, fall, and get up.

9. Habits are not eliminated, but replaced; hence, you need to replace pornography with a good habit. Keep yourself busy. Expend your energy doing profitable things like exercise, running, gardening, DIY, reading, etc.

10. Keep yourself in company with other godly individuals. Commit more time to reading God's word and doing His work. When you do these, you will less likely entertain the thoughts of watching pornography.

11. Consider seeing a therapist if needed who can help you discover the underlying reasons why you might be struggling with pornography.

23

MY HUSBAND IS IMPOTENT. I AM SEXUALLY FRUSTRATED. HE REFUSES TO GET MEDICAL HELP BECAUSE OF HIS EGO. HOW DO I DEAL WITH THIS?

I mpotence (erectile dysfunction) is the inability to achieve an erection or maintain it until orgasm. It is one of the most common male sexual problems, affecting approximately 140 million men worldwide. It is estimated that half of all men between the ages of 40 and 70 suffer from erectile dysfunction (ED) to some degree.

Most men have occasional times when they have problems achieving an erection. e.g. when tired, stressed, distracted, or have drunk too much alcohol. For most men, it is only temporary, and an erection occurs most times when sexually aroused.

About 8 in 10 cases of ED are due to a physical cause.

Causes of ED:

Reduced blood flow to the penis due to narrowed arteries. This is, by far, the most common cause of ED in men over the age of 40. The blood flow may then not be enough to cause an erection. Risk factors can increase your chance of narrowing the arteries. These include getting older, high blood pressure, high cholesterol, and smoking.

Diabetes - This is one of the most common causes of ED. Diabetes can affect blood vessels and nerves.

Nerve damage caused by multiple sclerosis, a stroke, Parkinson's disease, etc. can affect the nerves going to the penis.

Hormonal causes, e.g. a lack of a hormone called testosterone made in the testicles (testes). This is uncommon. Symptoms of a low testosterone level include a reduced sex drive (libido) and mood changes.

Side-effect of certain medications like some antidepressants; beta-blockers such as propranolol, atenolol, and diuretics (cimetidine). Alcohol and drug abuse, cycling.

Mental health (psychological) causes:

Performance anxiety can cause or contribute to ED. For instance, many men have occasional times when they cannot get or maintain an erection. If you have one episode where you can't have sexual intercourse; as a result, you may get anxious that it will happen again. This anxiety can be enough to stop you from getting an erection next time, leading to more anxiety.

Stress can be due to a difficult work or home situation, anxiety, relationship difficulties, and depression. Typically, the ED develops quite suddenly if it is a symptom of a mental health problem. The ED may resolve when your mental state improves - for example, if your anxiety or depression eases.

Erectile dysfunction can cause feelings of low self-esteem, anxiety, or depression. It can make a man depressed, angry, less masculine (the fact that they may see this as a symbol of their fertility and manliness and they're not able to achieve it on demand), socially isolated, in denial, lacking in self-confidence, and have the desire to avoid their spouse.

It also affects the mental health of a person's partner, making her feel confused, anxious, undesirable, or suspicious that their partner may be unfaithful. These feelings can put strain on a relationship. ED can also be difficult to talk about due to shame or stigma, preventing couples from communicating openly about it.

There are four ways couples approach the problem:

1. Some couples have a strong desire to resolve it.
2. Some admit there is a problem but decide not to seek treatment to resolve it.
3. Some refuse to admit or discuss it.
4. Some women feel angry that they not only withdraw, but may demean their partner or seek intimacy elsewhere.

Treatment options:

1. Being able to talk about it is the first step in resolving the problem. Open communication is crucial. Talking about it defuses any anger and frustration there may be, so that it doesn't spill over to other aspects of the relationship. Choose the right time to talk about it before you do it.
2. Explore other ways of maintaining physical intimacy, e.g. manual stimulation, stroking, kissing, cuddling etc. These can lead to orgasm in both partners. Couples, at times, are reluctant to explore any kind of physical contact for fear of further disappointment. That can lead to even more of a physical distance between the couple, which can eventually take its toll on the relationship. Focus on creating closeness rather than on penetration.

3. Counselling is beneficial. Individual counselling can give someone a private, non-judgmental space to talk about their difficulties and manage feelings of stress, anxiety, and low self-esteem. Couple's counselling may also be beneficial. In the majority of men with stress-related ED, their symptoms improve when their partner attends therapy with them. Counselling can help the couple learn how to communicate with and support each other, and it may help resolve any relationship problems that could be affecting sexual intimacy. A partner can cope by remembering that ED is often not personal and can discuss with a counsellor how their partner's ED makes them feel.

4. Lifestyle changes such as: weight loss, increasing exercise, eliminating alcohol intake, and stop smoking, etc.

5. Medical treatment: ED is usually treatable, most commonly by a tablet taken before sex. Non-invasive, like oral medications such as sildenafil (Viagra), injectable medications, such as alprostadil (Caverject), suppositories that a person inserts into the urethra, testosterone therapy for low testosterone levels, vacuum devices that draw blood into the penis, making it possible to maintain an erection temporarily.

6. Invasive surgery such as penile implant surgery.

7. Stopping any medication that might be causing

ED as a side effect and changing this medication may also be an option. It is essential always to discuss this with a doctor first.

WHY DID MY HUSBAND HAVE AN AFFAIR? CAN MY MARRIAGE SURVIVE IT?

M arital infidelity is one of the most hurtful things a couple can experience and the most difficult to get through.

Proverbs 5:15-20 (NKJV): *"Drink water from your own cistern, and running water from your own well. Should your fountains be dispersed abroad, streams of water in the streets? Let them be only your own, and not for strangers with you. Let your fountain be blessed, and rejoice with the wife of your youth. As a loving deer and a graceful doe, let her breasts satisfy you at all times; and always be enraptured with her love. For why should you, my son, be enraptured by an immoral woman, and be embraced in the arms of a seductress?"*

Hebrews 13:4 (NKJV): *"Marriage is honorable among all, and the bed undefiled; but fornicators and adulterers God will judge."*

There are diverse reasons men have affairs in marriage.

When a spouse is cheating, there is a possibility that their needs are not being met in the marriage. Men want to feel appreciated, admired, and loved by their wives. If they feel ignored or nagged at constantly they will seek someone else who listens, admires, compliments them, and makes them feel good instead of what they felt like with their own spouse.

If they are not happy in the marriage, they don't express these feelings to their spouses. Some get unsatisfied with the state of things and try to get what they need through cheating instead of communicating openly with their spouses. Some are happy to keep their wife and mistress.

Another reason for cheating is a spouse having unrealistic expectations of his spouse. He expects the wife to meet his every urge and sexual desire, not considering how she feels at any particular moment, or he may expect that their sex life will always be great, no matter what.

Some men cheat due to insecurity and immaturity. He may feel he is not handsome enough, or rich enough, or he may feel too old or whatever to be desirable. To bolster his ego, he has an affair to feel better about himself, reassure himself that he is still desirable, worthy, and wanted. This is often associated with a mid-life crisis.

Feeling immature can also be another reason. He thinks as long as his wife doesn't find out, he is not hurting her. That is far from the truth. The wife will eventually find out what's been going on. Women are intuitive beings.

Boredom in marriage, physical and emotional loneliness, plus laziness (not making an effort to work on the marriage) are conditions that can fuel adultery. At times, a man may cheat to get revenge (anger, resentment). He is angry and has resentment towards his spouse, and seeks to hurt her. Some have a desire for adventure and thrill, while others cheat to escape from the routine and blandness of everyday life; including their responsibilities and duties.

There are many different dynamics at play: timing, social and emotional connection to a spouse, happiness in marriage, and commitment to marriage.

Underneath all the various reasons for cheating, lies selfishness. **Proverbs 6:32-33 (NKJV):** *"Whoever commits adultery with a woman lacks understanding; He who does so destroys his own soul. Wounds and dishonor he will get, and his reproach will not be wiped away."*

It is the ongoing pattern of secrets and lies that surrounds cheating and the profound betrayal of trust that causes a loving spouse the most pain.

If your husband is cheating, he has made a conscious choice to. He didn't have to do it. No reason justifies his unfaithfulness to you.

Having an affair does not spell the end of your marriage. Your relationship can be restored, and perhaps even become stronger after the affair.

Yes, your marriage can thrive after an affair.

Some couples find a way to push the infidelity under the carpet and continue as if nothing happened. Some emerge from the trauma and infidelity stronger and happier than ever before. Some lead to divorce.

The only way a marriage can survive infidelity is if both spouses are willing to play their part to repair and recreate the marriage.

The first step in recovery from an affair is realising that it involves a lot of work, effort and time invested into it.

Repentance by the spouse who had the affair is paramount. **1 John 1:9 (NKJV):** *"If we confess our sins, He is faithful and just to forgive us our sins and to cleanse us from all unrighteousness.",* Also, forgiveness from the betrayed spouse set the foundation for marriage repair work.

The unfaithful spouse must take full responsibility for his or her choice to have an affair. It is not enough for the spouse to regret what he or she did and feel remorseful (feeling a deep sadness) over the affair. Repentance is not just about thoughts and emotions but about a change of behaviour. True repentance does not give excuses or apportion blame. It admits guilt, acknowledges the hurts caused, and it involves carefully looking at how the affair happened. It also works on breaking off the affair and genuinely resolve never to repeat it, or anything similar.

Forgiveness of an unfaithful spouse is one of the hardest kinds of forgiveness. *Ephesians 4:32*; **Romans 12:19-21 (NKJV)**: *"Beloved, do not avenge yourselves, but rather give place to wrath; for it is written, "Vengeance is Mine, I will repay," says the Lord.*

Therefore "If your enemy is hungry, feed him; If he is thirsty, give him a drink; For in so doing you will heap coals of fire on his head."

Do not be overcome by evil, but overcome evil with good."

Forgiveness is not instant and may take a long time to forgive the spouse fully. Unresolved hurts relating to the affair may spring up from time to time, long after the affair is over. Trust needs to be reestablished. Forgiveness is a decision the betrayed spouse chooses to make. The unfaithful spouse must be empathetic, patient and understanding towards the betrayed spouse and his/her struggle to make sense of things now. To bring up the affair repeatedly by the betrayed spouse is unhelpful and stalls the marriage's progress, so also is using the affair to shame the unfaithful spouse.

It's been noted that there is a big difference in healing time between "disclosed infidelity" and "discovered infidelity." It is much better for the betrayed partner to be told about the affair instead of discovering it accidentally. At times, the betrayed spouse may want to repeatedly hear the details of what happened and how the affair evolved. It is crucial that the spouse honestly answers all these questions. This improves the healing process.

Allow your spouse time to grieve. There is no part of the person physical, spiritual, mental, and emotional that is not deeply affected by the betrayal. Grief does not have a timeline. When a spouse forgives, it does not mean that all feelings of grief disappear. However, continue to move forward on the journey of recovery.

The couple needs to navigate through the initial crisis, steering through the various overwhelming emotions involved.

It takes courage to face your spouse and map out a recovery plan that involves repair, reconciliation and commitment. Rebuilding trust and security is a long-term process.

The couple must be open to counselling. The journey of recovery and restoration is a difficult, multifaceted one that needs navigation with the help of a counsellor. The role of a counsellor is to ask questions, mediate conflicts, and offer practical guidelines.

Be open to listening and acknowledging wrong. Recognise harmful and unhelpful behavioural patterns which existed in the marriage before the affair, which may have directly or indirectly contributed to the affair. There are always lessons to be learnt.

Recognise negative relationship patterns, identify what needs to change in the marriage, commit to positive change, and establish new behaviour patterns.

Rediscover your spouse's love language and commit to expressing it to him or her. *Refer to Question 1.*

Be accountable to a trustworthy person, e.g. a friend, your pastor or mentor, who will keep you in check. Accountability ensures that you follow through with the commitments and behaviours you have put in your marriage restoration journey.

25

IS COURTSHIP FOR SIX MONTHS ENOUGH TO CONSIDER MARRIAGE?

I n attempting to answer this question, I don't want to put a specific time frame of courtship as each couple is unique with their specific circumstances and peculiarities.

I would say wisdom is profitable to direct in the matter. In determining how short or long a courtship should last, several factors need to be considered, e.g. their geographical location, age, financial status, maturity, prevailing circumstances, etc.

The purpose of courtship is for a dating couple to see whether they are compatible for marriage. During courtship, a person gets to know more about the other person. They see them in different scenarios, with friends and family and in different seasons of the year. They get to know their likes and dislikes and their pet peeves (any annoying habits). They ask each other questions, explore their background, learn about their family, and spend time together. I am not sure these can be effectively accomplished within six months. People are able to put up their best behaviour for a few months, but a year will be hard to achieve. The longer the courtship period, the more you get to know about the person. I would say at least a year or longer.

For more information about courtship and the guidelines read my book, *10 Relationship Commandments Collection*.

A brief courtship creates a greater risk of a couple not knowing each other as well as they should or not resolving personal or relational issues that need to be settled before embarking on marriage. Seek God's guidance on your decision.

The scriptures say in the multitude of counsellors there is safety. **Proverbs 15:22 (NKJV):** *"Without counsel, plans go awry, but in the multitude of counselors they are established".*

Seek wise, godly counsel from spiritually trustworthy people who know and love you both. This might be parents, pastors, mentors, mature and trustworthy friends, or a professional counsellor. Don't be in haste to tie the knot just because you 'love' each other. There is much more to marriage than just love. If there are any 'red flags' in your relationship, deal with them now before they deal with you after marriage. Many marital problems were once premarital problems that were ignored or not taken seriously. Most importantly, seek God's wisdom and guidance through prayerfully asking for direction concerning your relationship.

26

WHY SHOULD I NOT MARRY SOMEONE OF A DIFFERENT RELIGION OR WHO IS IRRELIGIOUS?

The scriptures clearly states that we should not be unequally yoked with those of a different faith to us or of no faith, who are called unbelievers of the Christian faith. **2 Corinthians 6:14 (NKJV):** *"Be ye not unequally yoked together with unbelievers: for what fellowship hath righteousness with unrighteousness? and what communion hath light with darkness?"* A yoke is a device used to join two work animals for a common purpose, such as pulling a plough, Thus, be "yoked together" with another person means being united or joining that person for a common purpose.

When a Christian marries a non-Christian, they are *"unequally yoked together"* with an unbeliever. This is not God's will because there is a clear conflict in doctrine etc. Interfaith marriages tend to have many of issues due to tussles of who to worship, when, festivals, ceremonies, children's faith and much more.

Who you marry is the most important choice you will make next to accepting Jesus Christ as Lord and Saviour. It will affect how happy or unhappy you are, how easily you can serve God, how your children will be brought up, your peace, fulfilment of purpose and many other things Though there is no perfect marriage, a marriage between two Christians stands a greater chance of success since their shared belief in God provides a bedrock for the shared values that define their relationship. Spiritual foundation is the most important foundation because it affects other aspects of life and oneness in marriage. For a Christian, it is important that our spouses belong to the kingdom of God and share the same eternal destiny. **Amos 3:3 (NLT)** says, *"Can two people walk together without agreeing on the direction?"*

A marriage with a person of another religion or none poses potential problems and issues: conflict of interests, compromise of values, ideals, priorities, motivation, conformity to worldly standards, children upbringing issues, changes in you over time, conversion attempt failure and commitment to Christ decline, to name a few.

Why risk a life of heartache, loneliness, lack of spiritual bonding with your spouse and contentions based on your faith and belief? I don't think it's worth it!

Why would you want to consider marrying a person of another religion or none, when all the stakes are high? I believe your desire is to please God with all your heart and being, even in marriage.

27

I AM IN LOVE WITH A GUY WHO HAS AS GENOTYPE, MY GENOTYPE IS AA. SHOULD I BE WORRIED FOR WHEN WE HAVE CHILDREN?

What is a genotype?

A genotype is the entire genetic constitution in the red blood cells of an individual, i.e., the genetic makeup of an organism with reference to a single trait, set of traits, or an entire complex of traits. In a nutshell: your genotype is your complete heritable genetic identity; the sum total of genes transmitted from parent to offspring. There are four haemoglobin genotypes in humans: AA, AS, SS and AC. AC is uncommon. SS and AC are the abnormal genotypes or the sickle cells. We all have a specific pair of these haemoglobin in our blood which we inherited from both parents.

Why it is important to know your genotype:

Knowing one's haemoglobin genotype before choosing a life partner is important, because there may be compatibility issues that could have harmful effects on conception. People who are incompatible based on their genotype have a significant risk of giving birth to a child with sickle cell disease (a recessive disorder) This is a profoundly serious medical condition that significantly reduces the lifespan and makes a person struggle physically, with high prevalence rates in Africa South of the Sahara. Individuals with sickle cells experience severe pains in body parts where oxygen flow is compromised due to blockage in the blood vessels.

Sickle cell disease can only be inherited. It is not contagious and cannot be passed from one person to other. This disease only gets passed down from parents to children.

Those who struggle with sickle cells usually inherit two abnormal haemoglobin cells, and these are S. So basically, if both parents have S in their genotype, there is a chance of them giving birth to the child with haemoglobin SS genotype or sickle cell anaemia.

See the genotype compatibility chart:

www.facebook.com/kchgroup/posts/genotype-compatibilitygenotype-can-be-simply-defined-as-the-genetic-constitution/2264226190297708/

MEDICAL GENOTYPE TABLE FOR INTENDING COUPLES

Genotype Partner X	Genotype Partner Y	Possible Combinations				Remarks
AA	AA	AA	AA	AA	AA	CAN MARRY
AA	AS	AA	AS	AA	AS	CAN MARRY
AS	AS	AA	AS	AS	SS	NOT TO MARRY
SS	AA	AS	AS	AS	AS	CAN MARRY
SS	SS	SS	SS	SS	SS	NOT TO MARRY
AS	SC	SS	AS	AC	SC	NOT TO MARRY
AS	CC	AC	AC	SC	SC	NOT TO MARRY
AA	SC	AS	AC	AS	AC	CAN MARRY
AA	CC	AC	AC	AC	AC	CAN MARRY

Note: Three major groups of genotype are: AA (Normal); AS (Carrier), SS (Sickler). Others are SC and CC.

AA marries AA - That's the best compatibility. That way you save your future children the worry of genotype compatibility.

AA marries AS - your children will have AA and AS which is good. But sometimes, all your children may be AS which limits their future choice of partner.

AS and AS should not marry as there is every chance of having a child with SS.

AS and SS should not marry.

SS and SS must not marry since the children will have sickle cell disease.

The most common advice given to carriers of the sickle cell gene (AS, SS, SC) is not to marry fellow sickle cell gene carriers.

Those people with AS, SS, and SC genotypes are advised to marry only AA genotype to avoid the possibility of having SS babies.

Sickle-cell disease is the name of a group of inherited health conditions that affect the red blood cells, the most serious type is sickle-cell anaemia.

People with sickle cell disease produce unusually shaped red blood cells that cause problems because they don't look as long as healthy blood cells and can block blood vessels.

Sickle cell crisis (episodes of pain) is the most common and distressing of symptoms. They happen when blood vessels to some parts of the body become blocked. The pain can be so severe and lasts for up to seven days. It affects the hand and feet ribs, spine, pelvis, tummy, legs and arms.

The frequency of the pain episodes varies a lot (one every few weeks, one every year or less). Possible triggers are weather, i.e., wind, cold, rain, dehydration, stress, or strenuous exercise.

- More vulnerable to infections, e.g. colds, meningitis etc.

- Anaemia - headaches, dizziness, palpitations, etc.

Other symptoms are delayed growth during childhood, bone and joint pain, gall stones, persistent and painful erection of penis (priapism), strokes, acute chest syndrome (fever, cough, chest pain, and breathing difficulties).

Swelling of spleen, eyesight problems, blurred vision, high blood pressure, kidney problems, bedwetting, etc.

Treatment is lifelong:

It includes avoiding possible triggers of painful episode (sickle cell crisis), pain killers, hydroxyurea, long-term use of antibiotics, folic acid, stem cell or bone marrow transplants.

Some with this disease don't live long; however, many live long and fruitful lives due to advancement in medicine and knowledge of the disease.

28

DO INTERRACIAL AND INTERETHNIC MARRIAGES WORK?

Interracial and interethnic marriages can be successful but require a lot of work and effort from both parties. My marriage is a living example of a successful interethnic marriage. Every marriage has its challenges, including mixed marriages. The racial and cultural differences in a marriage won't necessarily cause a relationship to fail. What can cause it to fail is the inability of a couple to handle their differences and a failure to communicate their perspectives, and, any difficulties they are encountering.

A mixed marriage built on a solid foundation will surely stand the test of times. Such couples need to understand their differences, cultures, expectations, and family expectations. When you marry your spouse, you marry his/her family. When both spouses' parents approve of their union and welcome the son and daughter-in-law into their family, this goes a long way towards putting the marriage on a firm foundation. Family support is crucial as family rejection is more likely in mixed-race unions.

When two people from different cultures marry, an important key to making the union successful is respecting each other's cultural heritage. Our culture shapes us. By the time we are seven years old, we have imprinted certain belief systems. It is vital that two people of different races, cultures, nationalities, or ethnicities decide on boundaries, and guidelines.

When a spouse looks down on their spouse's culture as inferior to their own, or their ways and traditions, there is little chance of long-term happiness in the marriage. By disrespecting your spouse's culture, you disrespect your spouse, devaluing them as a person. If you show interest in their heritage, build relationships with his or her family, and see value in their way of doing things, your spouse feels accepted and honoured.

Discuss cultural differences regarding religion, parenting styles, grief, finances, diet, sex, extended family relationships, gender roles, communication styles, and traditions.

Discuss how you will raise your children and help them to understand and appreciate their mixed identity. Tell them positive stories of both of your family histories. As they grow up, listen to them as they share their concerns. They may experience prejudice and discrimination.

Be proud of your cultural traditions and work together to create ways to celebrate them that will be meaningful to you both.

Common possible challenges:

1. Different expectations.
2. Poor communication, e.g. different cultures communicate differently. Your partner may interpret what you say and feel differently than you meant it.
3. Family disapproval.
4. Societal judgement and negative attitudes.
5. Language barrier.
6. Lack of compromise.
7. Negative stereotyping.
8. Open hostility and intimidation.
9. A sense of isolation, loss of contact with friends and family that disapprove.
10. Rejection from family.

How to overcome some of these challenges:

1. Ensure your marriage has a solid foundation based on Christ.
2. Appreciate each other's differences and make room for compromises. The biggest enemy of

any relationship is a lack of compromise. You can't always have things your way. However, don't compromise your faith which is the bedrock of the relationship.

3. Communication is paramount. Don't make assumptions about your spouse based on their race. Rather understand each other's perspective. Make sure that whenever there is an issue, you address it immediately.

4. Be your authentic self.

5. Keep learning from each other and teaching each other.

6. Share your experiences with others who are in interracial/interethnic marriages.

7. Cultivate closer relationships with supporters of your union. This enhances happiness in the marriage.

8. Defend your spouse against loved ones who speak judgementally about them or the relationship (may not be easy to do!).

9. Find ways to express appreciation for your spouse's culture, such as learning their language, cooking traditional cultural dishes, conveying admiration etc.

While being in an interracial/intercultural marriage has its challenges, there are benefits too. You are exposed to the beauties of two cultures. You get to travel and meet new people along the way, eat different types of food, perhaps learn a different language, and much more. Such a marriage makes you become more open-minded, accommodating and understanding of others. It creates an amazing opportunity for personal growth. Accepting each other's differences and harnessing them, showing an interest in their heritage, building relationships with their people and seeing value in their way of doing things can be a deeply enriching experience. Your thriving interracial/intercultural marriage can be a testament that love triumphs everything.

In answer to your question, "do interracial and interethnic marriages work?" Yes, they can!

29

I AM EXPERIENCING ABUSE IN MY MARRIAGE. WHAT DO I DO?

Proverbs 6:16-19 (NKJV): *"These six things the Lord hates, Yes, seven are an abomination to Him:*
A proud look, A lying tongue, Hands that shed innocent blood, A heart that devises wicked plans, Feet that are swift in running to evil, A false witness who speaks lies, And one who sows discord among brethren."

The first thing that I would advise is that you seek help. You are not alone. I would also advise that you leave the environment you are in for a time, to separate you from the abusive relationship, and ensure your safety and well-being. Your safety and the safety of your children (if any) are paramount. Please, don't wait for an emergency to occur before acting! Don't suffer in silence. Whether you are male or female, help is available!

Let's explore in depth what domestic abuse is and what help is available to the victims and perpetrators.

What is domestic abuse?

The UK Government defines domestic abuse (also called domestic violence) as: any incident or pattern of incidents of controlling, coercive or threatening behaviour, violence or abuse between those aged 16 or over who are or have been intimate partners or family members regardless of gender or sexuality. This can encompass but is not limited to the following types of abuse:

- Psychological
- Physical
- Sexual
- Financial
- Emotional

Controlling behaviour is: a range of acts designed to make a person subordinate or dependent by isolating them from sources of support, exploiting their resources and capacities for personal gain, depriving them of the means needed for independence, resistance and escape and regulating their everyday behaviour.

"Coercive behaviour is: an act or a pattern of acts of assault, threats, humiliation and intimidation or other abuse that is used to harm, punish, or frighten their victim."

www.gov.uk/government/news/new-definition-of-domestic-violence

According to the National Domestic Violence Hotline statistics, one in four women and one in seven men over the age of 18 have been victims of physical violence and 50% of both sexes for psychological aggression. Anyone forced to change their behaviour because they are frightened of their partner or ex-partner's reaction is experiencing abuse.

Domestic abuse can happen to anyone of any race, age, sexuality, religion, or gender. It can occur within a range of relationships, including married couples, living together or dating. Domestic violence affects people of all socioeconomic backgrounds and education levels.

Anyone can be a victim of domestic violence, regardless of age, race, gender, sexual orientation, faith or class.

Domestic abuse is never the fault of the person who is experiencing it. Domestic abuse is a crime.

Domestic abuse includes:

- Constantly checking where someone is.
- Telling them they are ugly, too fat/thin, stupid, or useless.
- Treating them as a servant/slave.
- Constantly putting someone down or criticising them (for example, telling them they are a bad wife/mother).
- Preventing them from seeing friends or family.
- Not letting them get a job, or making them work long hours, or taking control of their wages.
- Not letting them leave the children alone, or not allowing them to touch or go near the children.
- Shouting, smashing things, throwing things, or sulking.
- Hitting, pushing, slapping, kicking and punching.
- Threatening to hurt someone they care about, such as children or pets.
- Rape, or making someone do sexual things they don't want to do.
- Humiliating someone through 'sexting' (sexual messages and images sent by mobile phone) or revenge pornography (posting private sexual material online).
- Using psychological abuse to make a woman

believe the abuse is her fault (sometimes called 'gas-lighting').

- Stalking and harassment (including online and texting or constantly calling).
- Using scripture to justify behaviour, for example, "I'm the head of the house and you have to submit to me".
- Not giving them any money, taking all their money from them, or checking exactly what they pay for.

Everyone has the right to feel safe, but domestic abuse sets up and thrives on fear.

Extract from a resource toolkit from the Black Church Domestic Abuse Forum (BCDAF).

Statistics show most domestic abuse is carried out by men and experienced by women.

UK's crime statistics for 2018 shows: on average two women were killed by their partner or ex-partner every week in England and Wales. *Office for National Statistics. Domestic abuse in England and Wales, year ending March 2018. Chapter 11: Domestic abuse related specific crime types.*

*where genders were recorded, 93% of prosecutions were against men and 83.7% of victims were women. *Crown Prosecution Service. Violence against women and girls report, 2017-18, A11.*

The most repeated and severe forms of abuse are carried out by men. In the UK crime statistics for 2015-2017, while 81% (283) of female murder victims were killed by a partner or ex-partner, the same figure for male victims was 13% (45).

Office for National Statistics, Crime statistics, focus on violent crime and sexual offences, year ending March 2017, p.18.

Abuse victims between the ages of 35 years to 49 years the greatest risk of being killed.

Men can experience domestic abuse - by either men or women. UK crime statistics for 2017-18 showed that 1.3 million women and 695,000 men had suffered some form of domestic abuse.

Office for National Statistics, Crime statistics, focus on violent crime and sexual offences, year ending March 2018, Chapter 11: Domestic abuse related specific crime types.

(Culled from a resource toolkit from the Black Church Domestic Abuse Forum {BCDAF}, www.bcdaf.org.uk)

The UN has described the worldwide increase in domestic abuse as a "shadow pandemic" alongside COVID-19.

It's thought cases have increased by 20% during the lockdown, as many people are trapped at home with their abuser.

June 2020, www.bbc.co.uk/news/av/world-53014211

Abuse cuts across all ethnic and economic backgrounds and occurs even in faith communities. In some cultures, women feel pressured to keep problems within the home and keep the family together at all costs.

Some fear they will lose face in the community if they leave. Abusers may threaten the victim with deportation. Isolation can be a factor for women who don't work outside the home. They may have less access to financial resources and information about domestic violence. Women with disabilities and elderly females are more vulnerable.

Domestic violence is often shrouded in silence. People outside the family may hesitate to interfere. Even extended family, out of loyalty to the abuser, can deny that abuse to protect the family's image.

Sometimes, even when domestic violence is reported, there are failures to protect the victims adequately or punish the perpetrators.

Why do men abuse?

Domestic violence is a mostly learned behaviour. Men learn to abuse through observations, experience, and reinforcement. They believe they have the right to use violence. They are rewarded; that is, their behaviours give them power and control over their partner.

Abusive men come from all economic classes, races, religions and occupations. The abuser may be a good provider and a respected member of his Church and community.

Abusive men share some common characteristics, such as, being extremely jealous, possessive and easily angered. They deny abuse is happening, or they minimise it. They often blame their abusive behaviours on someone or something other than themselves. They tell their spouse, "You made me do this".

They see women as inferior. Their conversations and language reveal their attitudes towards a woman's place in society. They believe men are to dominate and control women. Alcohol and drugs are often associated with domestic violence.

Why do the abused women stay in the relationship?

1. They stay with their abuser primarily out of fear. Some fear they will lose their children. They can't support themselves and their children. At times, they explain away his behaviour and believe that they can stop the abuse if they themselves act differently. Some are ashamed to admit that the man they love is terrorising them. Some have suffered 'battered woman' syndrome. Serious, long-term domestic abuse can result in a mental disorder called 'battered woman' syndrome or 'battered wife' syndrome. With 'battered woman' syndrome, a woman may develop learned helplessness that causes her to believe she deserves the abuse and that she can't get away from it. In many cases, it is why women don't report their abuse to the police or avoid telling friends and family about what's really going on.

There are four stages that women who develop 'battered woman' syndrome typically go through:

1st stage - Denial: The woman is unable to accept that she's being abused, or she justifies it as "just being that once."

2nd stage - Guilt: She believes she has caused the abuse.

3rd stage - Enlightenment: In this phase, she realizes that she didn't deserve the abuse and acknowledges that her partner has an abusive personality.

4th stage - Responsibility: She accepts that only the abuser holds responsibility. In many cases, this is when she'll try to escape the relationship.

Some women in abusive relationships never make it past the first two or three stages, as domestic violence can be fatal.

2. If you are a victim of domestic abuse, this next statistic should not discourage you from acting and leaving. It's important we add it so that you are equipped with ample information.

Some women run a risk of being killed when they leave their abuser or seek help from the legal system. There is a huge rise in the likelihood of violence after separation. 41% (37 of 91) of women killed by a male partner/former partner in England, Wales and Northern Ireland in 2018 had separated or taken steps to separate from them. Eleven of these 37 women were killed within the first month of separation and 24 were killed within the first year. *The Femicide Census: 2018 findings, Annual Report on UK Femicides 2018.*

3. Some victims may choose to stay at this time because it seems safer to them; Ultimately they must make their own decisions about staying or leaving.

4. Shame, embarrassment, or denial. Perpetrators are often well respected or liked in their communities because they are charming and manipulative. This prevents people from recognising the abuse, and it isolates the woman further. The perpetrator often minimises, denies, or blames the abuse on the victim. Victims may be ashamed or make excuses to themselves and others to cover up the abuse.

5. The use of headship theology in spousal abuse is common. Some abusers take the biblical text about submission in **Ephesians 5:22 (NKJV):** *"Wives, submit to your own husbands, as to the Lord"* and distort it to support their right to abuse."

6. Some abusers also cite scriptures like **Matthew 6:14-15 (NKJV):** *"For if you forgive men their trespasses, your heavenly Father will also forgive you. But if you don't forgive men their trespasses, neither will your Father forgive your trespasses"* to insist their wives forgive them. A victim then feels guilty if she cannot do so. Forgiveness does not mean forgetting the abuse or pretending it did not happen.

7. Women and men in faith communities where divorce is shunned and shameful, often feel trapped in abusive marriages.

How can the Church respond to domestic abuse (please note that this applies to both men and women. However, in our example, we will use her/she)?

The five Rs of responding to domestic abuse

Recognise:

a. That abuse does happen in Christian relationships

b. The signs of power and control in a relationship

Respond:

a. "I believe you" is a helpful first response

b. Within your limitations, and the safeguarding framework (especially if children are involved)

Refer:

a. To the National Domestic Violence Helpline on 0808 2000 247

b. Or to local professionals. Go with her if you can

Record:

a. Dates/times/details of what has been said

b. Your actions and concerns

c. Keep the notes in a secure place

Release:

a. Understand she may need to leave the area and the Church

b. Keep her in your prayers

c. Consider offering your support to local domestic abuse refuges

(Culled from a resource toolkit from the Black Church Domestic Abuse Forum {BCDAF}), www.bcdaf.org.uk)

Do's when responding to victims

- Find a safe place to talk.
- Invite someone else – if the woman agrees.
- Allow her time to talk.
- Listen to what she has to say – and take it seriously.
- Believe her. This is probably the tip of the iceberg.
- Prioritise her safety and the safety of any children.
- Empower her to make her own decisions.
- Support and respect her choices, even if she initially chooses to return to the abuser. However, be ready to overrule this choice if children are unsafe.
- Give information about support agencies. If she wants this, offer to contact them on her behalf and do so in her presence. Or offer a safe, private place where she can contact them herself.
- Use the expertise of people who are properly trained.
- Reassure her that it is not her fault; she doesn't deserve this, and it's not God's will for her.
- Let her know that the abuser's behaviour is wrong and completely unacceptable.
- Be patient with her.
- Protect her confidentiality. Keep any

information in a secure place and consider coding it.

Don'ts

- Don't judge her or what she tells you.
- Don't make unrealistic promises.
- Don't suggest that she should 'try again'. Victims experience several incidents before seeking help.
- Never minimise the severity of her experience or the danger she is in.
- Don't react with disbelief, disgust or anger at what she tells you, or react passively.
- Don't ask her why she did not act in a certain way.
- Never act on her behalf without her consent or knowledge (unless children are involved).
- Don't expect her to make decisions quickly.
- Never make decisions for her or tell her what to do.
- Don't suggest couples counselling, family mediation, marriage courses or healthy relationships courses.
- Don't encourage her to forgive and take him back.
- Don't send her home with a prayer or directive to submit to her husband, or be a better Christian wife.

- Don't contact the person at home, unless she agrees.
- Don't endanger her by asking her partner for his side of the story.
- Don't pass on details about her or her whereabouts.
- Don't encourage her to become dependent on you, or become emotionally involved with her.

Do's and don'ts when responding to perpetrators

Do's

- Put the victim's, and children's safety first.
- If meeting him is appropriate, do so in a public place or in the Church with other people around.
- When not in his presence, pray for him. Ask God to help him stop his violence and live differently.
- Understand that he alone is responsible for his behaviour and that being abusive is his choice.
- Never lose sight of the abuse he has perpetrated. Be aware he may claim that he is also a victim.
- If he is still in the relationship, only speak to him if he has been arrested or challenged by other agencies.
- If he is no longer in the relationship, only speak to him if his partner is in a safe place and agrees.
- Stay alert to the danger he may pose to you, other people, the victim, her children, and her wider family.
- Research treatment programmes and services such as RESPECT to help him change his behaviour.
- Find ways to collaborate with the police,

probation, and other services to hold him accountable.

- Address any religious rationalisations he may offer.
- Name the abuse as his problem, not hers. Tell him only he can stop it. Offer or refer him for help.
- Take seriously any murder threats and inform the police, the victim, her children or her family.
- Share any concerns you have with a properly trained professional.

Don'ts

- Don't go to him to confirm the victim's story.
- Don't meet him alone and in private.
- Never approach him or let him know you know about his violence. This should only be done by a trained professional, with the victim's permission, when she is safely separated from him.
- Don't allow him to use religious excuses.
- Don't recommend couple counselling for him and his partner if there is violence in the relationship.
- Never give him any information about his partner or her whereabouts, if she has left him.
- Don't be taken in by his minimising the abuse, denying he was abusive or lying about the abuse.
- Never accept it if he blames the victim or anything or anyone else.
- Don't be taken in by his 'conversion' experience. If it's genuine, it will be a tremendous resource as he proceeds with accountability. If it isn't, it is another way of manipulating you, to stay in control.
- Don't advocate for the abuser to avoid the legal consequences of his violence.
- Don't provide a character witness for court.
- Don't forgive an abuser quickly and easily.

- Don't confuse his guilt, sadness or remorse with true repentance.
- Never just send him home with a prayer.

(Culled from a resource toolkit from the Black Church Domestic Abuse Forum {BCDAF} www.bcdaf.org.uk)

Psychotherapist Carolyn Holderread Heggen (1996), maintains that while Christians need to uphold the sanctity of marriage, they also need to understand God's permissive nature in those instances where a marriage covenant has already been broken because of the existence of violence and abuse. In her view, marital permanency is not more important than the sanctity and safety of a woman. (*Carolyn Holderread Heggen, "Religious Beliefs And Abuse," in Women, Abuse, and the Bible: How Scripture Can be Used to Hurt or Heal, ed. James R Beck and Catherine Clark Kroeger {Grand Rapids, Michigan, USA: Baker Books, 1996}, 26)*

Because Christian marriage is considered a covenant relationship, some Christian women face the dilemma of feeling compelled to remain committed to marriage despite being victims of domestic violence.

While divorce may not be a desirable option, it is sometimes necessary and is indeed a biblical option. In support of this, Theologian Catherine Clark Kroeger quotes from the NIV version of Malachi 2:16 as follows, "The man who hates and divorces his wife....does violence to the one he should protect." Kroeger goes on to ask why Christian abusers and their victims don't consider verses such as Proverbs 6:17-19, which lists seven things which God hates, "haughty eyes, a lying tongue, shed innocent blood, a heart that devises wicked plans, feet that hurry to run to evil, a lying witness who testifies falsely, and one who sows discord in a family." Kroeger asks why the Church compels victims to remain in marriages characterised by any of these seven qualities which God hates. Kroeger follows this question by insisting that it is too often the case that preservation of marriage is exalted as a higher good than a human life's safety. She claims this is not what the Bible supports. She concludes that the possibility of divorce reinforces the serious nature of the offence and should serve as an incentive for changing abusive conduct. *(Nason-Clark; Kroeger, No Place for Abuse: Biblical and Practical Resources to Counteract Domestic Violence, Downers Grove, Illinois, USA: Inter-Varsity Press, 2001, 131-132)*

Many Christians hold the sanctity of marriage covenant in higher esteem than the physical safety of women and children.

A phrase often quoted is "a marriage must be saved at all costs". Therefore, despite ongoing violence, some women are told by Church leaders and counsellors to be obedient, prayerful, to remain in the relationship, believing that the marriage covenant is sacred and must not be broken.

It is harmful in an abusive relationship to apply hope and patience in the absence of safety and intervention since the cycle of abuse will inevitably continue to worsen, unless the abuser repents, takes responsibility and seeks assistance.

Rarely is the abuser called to account for creating a home environment that is so oppressive, thereby making his to seek safety and peace elsewhere. Sadly, for some women, separation from the husband will also mean judgement, and lack of understanding by the Church community.

Ultimately, the woman's safety and that of her children are paramount!

Some helpful agencies numbers:

Support with domestic abuse for women:

National Emergency services:

Dial 999

National Domestic Violence Helpline 0808 2000 247 (24-hour freephone), run by Refuge and Women's Aid.

Refuge: *www.refuge.org.uk* Supports women, children and men with services including refuges.

Women's Aid: *www.womensaid.org.uk* Working to end domestic abuse against women and children.

Samaritans: 116 123 (24 hours) *www.samaritans.org* Someone to listen, whatever people are going through.

Support with domestic abuse for men:

Men's Advice Line 0808 801 0327
www.mensadviceline.org.uk info@mensadviceline.org.uk

For men experiencing domestic violence:

Respect 0808 802 4040 (for people who hurt the one they love), 0808 801 0327 (for male victims) *www.respect.uk.net* Works with perpetrators of domestic violence and male victims.

Support for children and young people:

ChildLine 0800 1111 *www.childline.org.uk* National helpline for children.

Outside the UK:

In the USA, the Domestic Violence Hotline is 1-800-799-SAFE (7233).

Domestic And Sexual Violence Response Team (DSVRT), Lagos State, Nigeria 08000333333 *www.dsvrtlagos.org*

Other international helplines may be found via *www.befrienders.org*

30

I AM A 39-YEAR-OLD CHRISTIAN LADY WHO DIVORCED FIVE YEARS AGO. CAN I REMARRY?

Marriage is designed by God for life. But sadly, it is not always so. **Malachi 2:16 (NKJV):** *"For the LORD God of Israel says That He hates divorce, For it covers one's garment with violence," Says the LORD of hosts. "Therefore take heed to your spirit, That you do not deal treacherously."* The Bible does not command divorce – it permits, regulates and limits divorce. The Bible allows divorce – in certain situations – because of the hardness of human hearts.

The Bible offers two reasons for women to seek divorce: unfaithfulness and desertion **Matthew 5:32 (NKJV):** *"But I say to you that whoever divorces his wife for any reason except sexual immorality causes her to commit adultery; and whoever marries a woman who is divorced commits adultery.",*

Matthew 19:9 (NKJV): *"And I say to you, whoever divorces his wife, except for sexual immorality, and marries another, commits adultery; and whoever marries her who is divorced commits adultery."*

1 Corinthians 7:10-16 (NKJV): *"Now to the married I command, yet not I but the Lord: A wife is not to depart from her husband.*

But even if she does depart, let her remain unmarried or be reconciled to her husband. And a husband is not to divorce his wife.

But to the rest I, not the Lord, say: If any brother has a wife who does not believe, and she is willing to live with him, let him not divorce her.

And a woman who has a husband who does not believe, if he is willing to live with her, let her not divorce him.

For the unbelieving husband is sanctified by the wife, and the unbelieving wife is sanctified by the husband; otherwise your children would be unclean, but now they are holy.

But if the unbeliever departs, let him depart; a brother or a sister is not under bondage in such cases. But God has called us to peace.

For how do you know, O wife, whether you will save your husband? Or how do you know, O husband, whether you will save your wife?"

Where there is violence, the sacred vow of marriage and oneness is broken by an abusive husband. The abuser destroys a marriage covenant when he abuses his wife. In essence he deserts her by his inappropriate abuse of behaviour.

Let's see what several other scriptures say on divorce and remarriage:

1 Corinthians 7:39 (NKJV): *"A wife is bound by law as long as her husband lives; but if her husband dies, she is at liberty to be married to whom she wishes, only in the Lord."*

Romans 7:2 (NKJV): *"For the woman who has a husband is bound by the law to her husband as long as he lives. But if the husband dies, she is released from the law of her husband."*

Luke 16:18 (NKJV): *"Whoever divorces his wife and marries another commits adultery; and whoever marries her who is divorced from her husband commits adultery."*

Mark 10:11-12 (NKJV): *"So He said to them, "Whoever divorces his wife and marries another commits adultery against her.*
And if a woman divorces her husband and marries another, she commits adultery."

Matthew 5:31-32 (NKJV): *"Furthermore it has been said, 'Whoever divorces his wife, let him give her a certificate of divorce.'*

But I say to you that whoever divorces his wife for any reason except sexual immorality causes her to commit adultery; and whoever marries a woman who is divorced commits adultery."

A question like yours is not easy to answer because the Bible does not go into great detail regarding different circumstances for remarriage after a divorce. There are different opinions among believers, theologians and denominations about the "rightness" or "wrongness" of remarriage after divorce.

In my opinion every case should be judged on its own merits.

Can you remarry or should you remarry is a question I cannot answer as I don't know the circumstances of your divorce five years ago or your current circumstances. I don't want to play judge or jury over your life. Your decision to remarry is a decision you must make yourself. I suggest you prayerfully seek counsel and biblical guidance from those who have spiritual authority over your life. **Proverbs 11:14 (NKJV):** *"Where there is no counsel, the people fall; but in the multitude of counselors there is safety."* Ultimately, the final decision is between you and God. Pray to God for guidance on what to do. **Proverbs 3:5-6 (NKJV):** *"Trust in the Lord with all your heart, And lean not on your own understanding; In all your ways acknowledge Him, And He shall direct your paths."* Don't be led by your feelings, or societal pressures. God is a faithful; He does not leave His children comfortless. Seek His wisdom and counsel on the matter. He will surely direct you.

CONCLUSION

A maximized marriage is a marriage in which husband and wife are continually working on their union, through different seasons and stages of life and, through 'thick and thin' with their ultimate aim of pleasing God till death part them.

Now that you have read through this book, I believe you have acquired some wisdom to apply in your marriage which you can even use to counsel others.

"A wise man will hear and increase learning, And a man of understanding will attain wise counsel," **Proverbs 1:5 (NKJV).**

No doubt, the tools, skills, and motivation in this book will help strengthen your marriage, rebuild, and restore it. It will also guide you in making wise choices on your marital journey. There are very few things that cannot be worked on in a marriage and even repaired and resolved. None of us can afford to leave God out of our relationships. Who is best to consult than the author and creator of marriage God!

Prayer to God is the master key. Prayer makes a difference. **Philippians 4:6-7 (NKJV):** *"Be anxious for nothing, but in everything by prayer and supplication, with thanksgiving, let your requests be made known to God; and the peace of God, which surpasses all understanding, will guard your hearts and minds through Christ Jesus."*

If this book has blessed you, please recommend it to other people, whether married or singles. You never know whose marriage or intending marriage you may be saving.

In life, there is no monopoly of wisdom. I am well aware that you may have some contrary opinions from mine in some answers. That is fine; nevertheless, I hope you will find many of the answers within this book beneficial. I have written several other books on marriage and relationships which you can further avail yourself of.

Please email me your views, comments, feedback and compliments at *info@gracesolaoludoyi.com*.

May God bless your marriage!

REFERENCES

Unless otherwise marked, all scripture quotations are taken from the New King James Version of the Holy Bible.

A resource toolkit from the Black Church Domestic Abuse Forum (BCDAF), *www.bcdaf.org.uk*

www.bbc.co.uk/news/av/world-53014211

The Femicide Census: 2018 findings. Annual Report on UK Femicides 2018

www.gov.uk/government/news/new-definition-of-domestic-violence

The 5 Love Languages® by Gary Chapman, © 2015, Northfield Publishing, *www.5lovelanguages.com*

Grace Oludoyi, I Pronounce You Husband and Wife!, Revised Edition, London: Baruch Press, 2015, pgs., 168-171

Grace Oludoyi, 10 Relationship Commandments, Designxpirit, UK, pgs., 124-125

John Gottman & Nan Silver, Why Marriages Succeed or Fail And How to Make Yours Last. Bloomsbury Publishing Plc, London W1D 3QY, 2007, pgs., 68-102

Genotype Chart by KCH Group,

www.facebook.com/kchgroup/posts/genotype-compatibilitygenotype-can-be-simply-defined-as-the-genetic-constitution/2264226190297708

www.kch.com.ng

Dave Willis;

www.marriagemissions.com/privacy-vs-secrecy-marriage

Nason-Clark; Kroeger, No Place for Abuse: Biblical and Practical Resources to Counteract Domestic Violence, Downers Grove, Illinois, USA: Inter-Varsity Press, 2001, pgs.,131-132

Carolyn Holderread Heggen, "Religious Beliefs And Abuse," in Women, Abuse, and the Bible: How Scripture Can be Used to Hurt or Heal, ed. James R Beck and Catherine Clark Kroeger, Grand Rapids, Michigan, USA: Baker Books, 1996, pgs.,26

Scott and Bethany Palmer, *www.themoneycouple.com*

Merriam-Webster.com dictionary

OTHER BOOKS
BY DR GRACE SOLA-OLUDOYI

I Pronounce You Husband and Wife!

I Pronounce You Husband and Wife! (revised edition)

Let Nothing Put Asunder! Unhealthy Games Men And
Women Play In Marriage

One Thing Led To Another! Unhealthy Games Singles Play
In Relationships

Woman to Woman: 15 Essentials of a Thriving Women's
Ministry

Trials of a Pastor's Wife

The Golden Seven: 7 Things Every Parent Owes Their Child

Ten Relationship Commandments Collection

50 Lessons Life Has Taught Me

OTHER PUBLICATIONS

12 Practical Ways to Soul Winning

ABC of Faith

To buy any of these books, go to:

www.GraceSolaOludoyi.com

or email: *drgraceoludoyiresources@gmail.com*

Printed in Great Britain
by Amazon

78225199R00104